ONLY
REMEMBERED

ONLY REMEMBERED

Compiled and Edited by MICHAEL MORPURGO

In aid of

Illustrated by Ian Beck

JONATHAN CAPE • LONDON

ONLY REMEMBERED
A JONATHAN CAPE BOOK 978 0 857 55128 3

Published in Great Britain by Jonathan Cape,
an imprint of Random House Children's Publishers UK
A Random House Group Company

This edition published 2014

1 3 5 7 9 10 8 6 4 2

Introduction copyright © Michael Morpurgo, 2014
Illustrations copyright © Ian Beck, 2014
Introductions and commentaries © individual contributors, 2014

Text and images copyright © individual authors and artists; see Acknowledgements

The Random House Group Limited supports the Forest Stewardship Council® (FSC®),
the leading international forest-certification organisation. Our books carrying the FSC label
are printed on FSC®-certified paper. FSC is the only forest-certification scheme supported
by the leading environmental organisations, including Greenpeace. Our paper procurement
policy can be found at www.randomhouse.co.uk/environment

MIX
Paper from
responsible sources
FSC® C016897

Set in Minion

RANDOM HOUSE CHILDREN'S PUBLISHERS UK
61–63 Uxbridge Road, London W5 5SA

www.randomhousechildrens.co.uk
www.totallyrandombooks.co.uk
www.randomhouse.co.uk

Addresses for companies within The Random House Group Limited can be found at:
www.randomhouse.co.uk/offices.htm

THE RANDOM HOUSE GROUP Limited Reg. No. 954009

A CIP catalogue record for this book is available from the British Library.

Printed and bound in Great Britain by Clays Ltd. St Ives plc

CONTENTS

AT HOME

AFTER

WHO'LL SING THE ANTHEM?
WHO WILL TELL THE STORY?

Some years ago I came across the grave of a young British soldier in France, one of thousands, one of hundreds of thousands. I had stopped to look, I think, because there was a wreath of poppies lying there. I read on the gravestone that this was a private killed in 1918, only two weeks before the end of the First World War. He was aged just twenty-one. On the wreath was written: *To my Grandpa. I never knew you, and I wish I had.* Out of the ten million soldiers who were killed on all sides, many were young, some barely out of school. Most never grew old enough to know and be known by their children or their grandchildren. This book is made for them; for all of them.

In my small village of Iddesleigh, in deepest Devon, there lives the last surviving widow of any of the soldiers who marched off from this country to the First World War. Her soldier was called Wilf Ellis. I knew him when he was an old man. And thereby hangs a tale, the terrible tale of the ten million soldiers, and of the ten million horses, all killed in the First World War.

Dorothy Ellis, now ninety-three, has lived quietly, and spent much of her life looking after the village church, keeping it clean and bright. Wilf now lies in the churchyard, as do other old men I once knew: Captain Budgett and Albert Weeks. But before they died they told me their stories.

When he came back from the war, Wilf Ellis played in dance bands on transatlantic liners before becoming an antique dealer in the village, 'a knocker'. I bought a picture from him once, an old oil painting of a racehorse standing in a stable. The horse was called Topthorn. Topthorn, as you will see, was later to play a part in this tale.

I didn't know Wilf Ellis well, just enough to talk to. Thirty-five years ago now, we met by chance in the pub, the Duke of York. We got talking by the log fire. I'd heard he'd been to the First World War as a young man, so I asked him about it. It was a conversation which very soon became a monologue. He told me how his uniform had made him itch when he first put it on. He talked of the trenches, the machine guns and the snipers, and the mud, and the whizz-bangs and the wire; how he was gassed and hospitalized, how his life was once spared by a German soldier, of the horses who died the same way as the soldiers, of going out on night patrols – his courage fuelled by rum – of the fear, of the joy of hot food and a communal hot bath, of the relief when it was all over.

I knew even when he was talking that he was passing his story on to me. Much of it, Dorothy later told me, he'd never spoken of before. And I was a comparative stranger. He took me to his cottage and showed me his trenching tool, some photographs of himself, of his pals. Before I met Wilf Ellis I had gleaned all I knew of the First World War from the poetry of Wilfred Owen and Sassoon and Edward Thomas and Blunden. I had seen the film and read the book of *All Quiet on the Western Front* by Remarque, and the film too of *Paths of Glory*, and the play, *Journey's End*, the musical of *Oh, What a Lovely War!* But now I had heard it face to face, from someone who had been there, who told it straight, all of it understated, with no artifice. This was simply his story.

Inspired to know more, a few days later I went to see Captain Budgett, 'the squire' of the village, ex-master of fox-hounds, my neighbour, and asked him about his time away at that war. He told me he was there 'with horses', and spoke of his horse as his best friend – he'd talk to him in the horse-lines at night, whisper in his ear and tell him his secret hopes and fears, and his horse had listened to him. I spoke to Albert Weeks, farm worker all his life, who hadn't been to the war, being too young, but who was there when the farm horses were sold off to the army on the village green in 1914, who saw his friends march away, some never to return; and who told me how the world was never the same afterwards.

So it was, with their stories in my head, that I was able to sit down and write my story, *War Horse*, the story of Albert, the young farm worker growing up on the farm near Iddesleigh with his beloved foal Joey, how Joey was sold away to the army as a cavalry horse and taken to France, only to be captured by the Germans, along with Topthorn, his stable companion and friend, after the first cavalry charge of the war. Through Joey's eyes we live through the universal suffering of that war as he saw it and knew it; we endure his pain, feel his longing for Albert and home. Further novels about the First World War followed, all inspired, I have no doubt, by the truth told to me by these old men: *Farm Boy*, the sequel to *War Horse*, *The Butterfly Lion* and *The Best Christmas in the World*.

It was the National Theatre that discovered *War Horse* – a book I loved but until then few had read – and turned it into a huge theatrical event, an iconic play now seen all over the world. I am pleased about that for all sorts of reasons, but mainly because indirectly, through the play and through the subsequent film, Joey's story, which is of course Wilf's story, Captain Budgett's story, Albert Weeks's story, has been passed on to millions, maybe even ten million. The anthem sung, the story told.

*

The title of this book, *Only Remembered*, is also the song that begins and ends the play of *War Horse*. It was written by John Tams, the great folk singer. Here is a verse of that song:

> *Only the truth that in life we have spoken,*
> *Only the seed that in life we have sown.*
> *These shall pass onwards when we are forgotten.*
> *Only remembered for what we have done.*

Here in this book you will find truth, which comes in many guises, in history, in stories, fictional and non-fictional, in poems and songs and pictures. My deepest thanks to those who have contributed, in particular to Annie Eaton, Ruth Knowles and Rachel Mann of Random House.

As for myself, I should like to offer, as my contribution to this collection, a piece translated from the French, from the book *On les Aura*, illustrated by Barroux. It comes from the recently discovered diary of an unknown French soldier as he goes off to war and into action in 1914. It is simply told, very much as Wilf Ellis and Captain Budgett and Albert Weeks told me their stories in the Duke of York pub in Devon all those years ago.

MICHAEL MORPURGO – Author

WEDNESDAY 5 AUGUST

This time, it's the great send-off. We're up at 04:00 hours because parade is at 05:00 hours. After collecting our haversacks filled with bread and a rabbit cooked the previous day, it's time for farewells.

All five of us shed a tear. After promising Madame Fernand that we'll stick together, we leave with heavy hearts, but our sense of duty makes us hold our heads high and soon we've joined the ranks, ready for the off.

The unknown soldier heads to the trenches

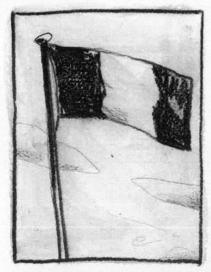

Once the regiment is on parade, the colonel has us salute the flag and he gives a rousing speech, which is met with cheers. Then we march to the station with the band playing.

07:00 hours: The train whistles and sets off in the direction of Paris. What a cruel irony! After a stop at Corbeil, the train departs again but this time heading eastwards. At the stations, the ladies from the Red Cross bring us food and drink. We pass though Montereau, Romilly and Troyes. Where are we going? Who knows.

From *Line of Fire: Diary of an Unknown Soldier*, Barroux

AT WAR

Goodbye-ee, Goodbye-ee

Brother Bertie went away
To do his bit the other day,
With a smile on his lips,
And his Lieutenant's pips,
Upon his shoulder bright and gay.
As the train pulled out he said,
'Remember me to all the birds.'
And he wagg'd his paw
And went away to war,
Shouting out these pathetic words:

'Goodbye-ee, goodbye-ee,
Wipe the tear, baby dear, from your eye-ee,
Tho' it's hard to part, I know,
I'll be tickled to death to go.
Don't cry-ee, don't sigh-ee,
There's a silver lining in the sky-ee,
Bonsoir old thing, cheerio, chin, chin,
Nap-poo, toodle-oo, Goodbye-ee.

If You Want the Old Battalion

If you want the old battalion,
I know where they are, I know where they are,
I know where they are,
If you want the old battalion, I know where they are,
They're hanging on the old barbed wire

I've seen them, I've seen them,
Hanging on the old barbed wire
I've seen them,
Hanging on the old barbed wire.

FROM *WAR HORSE*

Like all army horses we were clipped out like hunters so that all our lower quarters were exposed to the mud and rain. The weaker ones amongst us suffered first, for they had little resilience and went downhill fast. But Topthorn and I came through to the spring, Topthorn surviving a severe cough that shook his whole massive frame as if it was trying to tear the life out of him from the inside. It was Captain Stewart who saved him, feeding him up with a hot mash and covering him as best he could in the bleakest weather.

And then, one ice-cold night in early spring, with frost lying on our backs, the troopers came to the horse-lines unexpectedly early. It was before dawn. There had been a night of incessant heavy barrage. There was a new bustle and excitement in the camp. This was not one of the routine exercises we had come to expect. The troopers came along the horse-lines in full service order, two bandoliers, respiratory haversack, rifle and sword. We were saddled up and moved silently out of the camp and onto the road. The troopers talked of the battle ahead and all the frustrations and irritations of imposed idleness vanished as they sang in the saddle. And my Trooper Warren was singing along with them as lustily as any of them. In the cold grey of the night the squadron joined the regiment in the remnants of a little ruined village peopled only by cats, and waited there for an hour until the pale light of dawn crept over the horizon. Still the guns bellowed out their fury and the ground shook beneath us. We passed the field hospitals and the light guns before trotting over the support trenches to catch our first sight of the battlefield. Desolation and destruction were everywhere.

Not a building was left intact. Not a blade of grass grew in the torn and ravaged soil. The singing around me stopped and we moved on in ominous silence and out over the trenches that were crammed with men, their bayonets fixed to their rifles. They gave us a sporadic cheer as we clattered over the boards and out into the wilderness of no-man's-land, into a wilderness of wire and shell holes and the terrible litter of war. Suddenly the guns stopped firing overhead. We were through the wire. The squadron fanned out in a wide, uneven echelon and the bugle sounded. I felt the spurs biting into my sides and moved up alongside Topthorn as we broke into a trot. 'Do me proud, Joey,' said Trooper Warren, drawing his sword. 'Do me proud.'

Michael Morpurgo

Sketches from War Horse, *as drawn by Rae Smith*

DAME EVELYN GLENNIE – Percussionist

I have read so much about the incessant and monstrous din of warfare that constantly bombarded the soldier's body with the noise and vibration of bursting shells and caused great pain to their ears. The noise was so enormously resounding that rain and thunder became pleasant and soothing in comparison.

This set me thinking about whether, in my vast collection of over 1,800 percussion instruments, any might have been used by the actual soldiers during the First World War, and for what purpose? We know that percussion instruments produce high and low sounds, resonant and short sounds, and therefore, what would be the most effective to compete with their already noise-polluted environment?

We are aware of the use of drums in warfare and how the impact of striking a drum and being moved by rhythm can propel a sense of purpose and teamwork, injecting a sense of fearless determination. However, my eyes wander to my collection of whistles.

Yes, strange though it is, the whistle is given to the percussion player rather than the wind player, so it has always belonged to the percussion family. The whistle is used worldwide in sport, music, on ships, in hunting, by train guards and much more. However, whistles were also used in various military situations, mainly to initiate a pre-set plan so that all parts would act simultaneously. For example, officers in the First World War would sometimes blow whistles to signal all troops along a broad stretch of trench to attack at the same time.

The ratchet was another instrument used by soldiers, often to warn of the presence of poison gas or other type of attack.

The whistle and ratchet are small 'hand-held' instruments, crucial for the circumstances of the soldiers, considering they were in such confined spaces, but the sounds they made spliced through their heavily noise-bombarded environment.

It's fascinating to see, touch and play the many instruments at our disposal and to think of how they may have been used in the past, saving countless lives in the process.

SHAMI CHAKRABARTI – Director of Liberty

I first read this Wilfred Owen poem when a youth of fifteen or sixteen myself. I couldn't help but be touched by its special blend of beauty, anger and irony. Perhaps Owen was an original 'emo', exploring the contrast between the grand ceremony of militarism and religion, and the reality of doomed boys killed 'as cattle'.

ANTHEM FOR DOOMED YOUTH

What passing-bells for these who die as cattle?
Only the monstrous anger of the guns.
Only the stuttering rifles' rapid rattle
Can patter out their hasty orisons.
No mockeries now for them; no prayers nor bells;
Nor any voice of mourning save the choirs,
The shrill, demented choirs of wailing shells;
 And bugles calling for them from sad shires.

What candles may be held to speed them all?
Not in the hands of boys but in their eyes
Shall shine the holy glimmers of goodbyes.
The pallor of girls' brows shall be their pall;
Their flowers the tenderness of patient minds,
And each slow dusk a drawing-down of blinds.

Wilfred Owen

LORD PADDY ASHDOWN – Politician

Amongst the many unbearable tragedies about the First World War (indeed, any war), one of the most unbearable is the young men who volunteered because they thought that war was a glorious thing. It is, in fact, a muddy, bloody, terrible piece of insanity.

This poem tells a truth which tears away that ancient deception, so loved by kings and prime ministers and generals far behind the lines. It should be hung in every recruiting office and read out to every new recruit before he (or, nowadays, she too) signs up.

DULCE ET DECORUM EST

Bent double, like old beggars under sacks,
Knock-kneed, coughing like hags, we cursed through sludge,
Till on the haunting flares we turned our backs
And towards our distant rest began to trudge.
Men marched asleep. Many had lost their boots
But limped on, blood-shod. All went lame; all blind;
Drunk with fatigue; deaf even to the hoots
Of tired, outstripped Five-Nines that dropped behind.

Gas! Gas! Quick, boys! – An ecstasy of fumbling,
Fitting the clumsy helmets just in time;
But someone still was yelling out and stumbling,
And flound'ring like a man in fire or lime . . .

Dim, through the misty panes and thick green light,
As under a green sea, I saw him drowning.

In all my dreams, before my helpless sight,
He plunges at me, guttering, choking, drowning.

If in some smothering dreams you too could pace
Behind the wagon that we flung him in,
And watch the white eyes writhing in his face,
His hanging face, like a devil's sick of sin;
If you could hear, at every jolt, the blood
Come gargling from the froth-corrupted lungs,
Obscene as cancer, bitter as the cud
Of vile, incurable sores on innocent tongues, –
My friend, you would not tell with such high zest
To children ardent for some desperate glory,
The old Lie: *Dulce et decorum est*
Pro patria mori.

Wilfred Owen

FRANK FIELD – Politician

Wilfred Owen's poems, more than the work of any other poet or writer, changed the way we now view the First World War. But that to me is only part of his attraction. From the age of five, Wilfred lived in Birkenhead, a seat I have represented in parliament since 1979. When Wilfred was fourteen, his father, who was stationmaster at Woodside Station, gained a promotion to Shrewsbury. It was there, on Armistice Day in 1918, that a telegraph boy brought his mother a War Office telegram telling her that Wilfred had been killed a week earlier.

Our vision of what was called the Great War was shaken up, like a kaleidoscope, largely by the war poets. The huge sacrifices – three quarters of a million British dead alone – began to be seen as a huge deceit. Brave British soldiers had been led by donkeys to a mass slaughter. And for what?

At this point we lost connection with historical reality, and in its place the views of the war poets – of the senseless waste – took control. Owen's work was fundamental to this change.

I hope that this poem by a Birkenhead boy brings home the horror of any war, and the sheer bravery of so many of those participating. But we do have to ask why they were participating, and why they participated for so long.

So please do heed this health warning. The First World War, as the Great War was renamed once a second one was recorded on the pages of history, changed fundamentally the course of the twentieth century, and therefore the world in which we now live.

How we weigh the costs against the gains is a task of huge difficulty; any judgement will be finely balanced.

Be thrilled and shocked by the images Owen gives us of those terrible battles. But in doing so, please look to the gains as well as the losses that the world experienced in a war that I believe was, on balance, important to fight.

STRANGE MEETING

It seemed that out of the battle I escaped
Down some profound dull tunnel, long since scooped
Through granites which titanic wars had groined.

Yet also there encumbered sleepers groaned,
Too fast in thought or death to be bestirred.
Then, as I probed them, one sprang up, and stared
With piteous recognition in fixed eyes,
Lifting distressful hands, as if to bless.
And by his smile, I knew that sullen hall,
By his dead smile I knew we stood in Hell.

With a thousand pains that vision's face was grained;
Yet no blood reached there from the upper ground,
And no guns thumped, or down the flues made moan.
'Strange friend,' I said, 'here is no cause to mourn.'
'None,' said the other, 'save the undone years,
The hopelessness. Whatever hope is yours,
Was my life also; I went hunting wild
After the wildest beauty in the world,
Which lies not calm in eyes, or braided hair,

But mocks the steady running of the hour,
And if it grieves, grieves richlier than here.
For by my glee might many men have laughed,
And of my weeping something had been left,
Which must die now. I mean the truth untold,
The pity of war, the pity war distilled.
Now men will go content with what we spoiled,
Or, discontent, boil bloody, and be spilled.
They will be swift with swiftness of the tigress.
None will break ranks, though nations trek from progress.
Courage was mine, and I had mystery,
Wisdom was mine, and I had mastery:
To miss the march of this retreating world
Into vain citadels that are not walled.
Then, when much blood had clogged their chariot-wheels,
I would go up and wash them from sweet wells,
Even with truths that lie too deep for taint.
I would have poured my spirit without stint
But not through wounds; not on the cess of war.
Foreheads of men have bled where no wounds were.

I am the enemy you killed, my friend.
I knew you in this dark: for so you frowned
Yesterday through me as you jabbed and killed.
I parried; but my hands were loath and cold.
Let us sleep now . . .

Wilfred Owen

MALORIE BLACKMAN – Author and Children's Laureate 2013–2015

Walter Tull was born in Kent, the mixed-race son of a Barbadian carpenter and a white English mother. He played professional football for Tottenham Hotspur and Northampton Town before joining the British Army at the outbreak of the First World War.

The world has changed in many ways since then but, depressingly, much remains the same. The original Sherlock Holmes stories had Dr John Watson returning from a war in Afghanistan. A recent BBC modernization didn't have to change that detail at all. In 1914 the Balkans were a patchwork of small states with simmering ethnic tensions, and they still are. And when Walter Tull played football for Tottenham Hotspur, he was subjected to appalling racist abuse. Sadly, a century later, that still seems to be with us too.

But there is progress, and hope! Tull set the trend, not just as a black soldier, but as a black officer – a highly regarded black officer. In 1914, by the strict interpretation of British Military Law, he shouldn't even have been an officer at all. At the time army regulations stipulated that 'any negro or person of colour' was not allowed to become one. Despite this rule, Tull performed so impressively that in 1917 his superiors promoted him to the rank of lieutenant. This made him the first black or mixed-race officer in a British Army combat unit, and the first to lead white men into battle.

Tull and His Fellow Officers

Tull first fought in France and then in Italy from 1917–18. After he twice led his men on raids across the River Piave – and each time brought them back safely – Tull was cited for his 'gallantry and coolness' by his commanding general. He was, in fact, recommended for the Military Cross for his bravery, but he never received one.

On 25 March 1918, operating once again in France, Lieutenant Tull was ordered to lead his men in an attack on the German trenches. Soon after entering no-man's-land, Tull was hit by a German bullet. He was so popular that his men risked their own lives attempting to bring him back to the British trenches. But the

German machine-gun fire was too intense and they failed. Tull's body was never recovered and he is one of thousands of soldiers from the First World War who have no known grave.

One death is a tragedy. The sixteen million-plus deaths that occurred as a result of the First World War are not just a statistic, they are a catastrophe. Second Lieutenant Walter Tull fought against narrow-mindedness and bigotry all his life, but he also demonstrated what a brave heart and a fighting spirit can achieve.

Slowly we edge closer to the day Martin Luther King foresaw in his famous 'I have a dream . . .' speech. A day where people 'will not be judged by the colour of their skin, but by the content of their character'.

Walter Daniel John Tull
28 April 1888–25 March 1918

JULIAN BARNES – Writer

Siegfried Sassoon was an English poet naturally more interested in cricket than in politics, who joined up at the outbreak of war, fought very bravely, and was awarded the Military Cross. Then, appalled by the way the war was being run, and distraught at the death of a close friend, he wrote to his commanding officer refusing to return to the front after leave. His letter was read out in Parliament and caused a famous outcry.

But Sassoon's real and lasting protest – not just against the First World War, but against all war – came in the form of poetry. In short, savage, easily understood poems, he described the reality of war, the incompetence of leaders, the hypocrisy of the press, and the nauseating fireside jingoism of those who cheered on the slaughter from a distance. He was what nowadays we would call a whistle-blower – but a whistle-blower in verse.

This is his poem called 'The General':

THE GENERAL

'Good-morning; good-morning!' the General said
When we met him last week on our way to the line.
Now the soldiers he smiled at are most of 'em dead,
And we're cursing his staff for incompetent swine.
'He's a cheery old card,' grunted Harry to Jack
As they slogged up to Arras with rifle and pack.

But he did for them both by his plan of attack.

Siegfried Sassoon

BEN BARNES – Actor

When I was seventeen years old, I studied Pat Barker's *Regeneration* for my English A level. It resonated with me as an Englishman, but also as the son of a psychiatrist and psychotherapist.

Some of the scenes from the book came back to me a decade later, when I was rehearsing for the play *Birdsong*, which was based on another novel about the psychological impact on soldiers fighting in the First World War.

Barker's powerful novel focuses on the experiences of soldiers treated for shell shock at a war hospital in Edinburgh in 1917. At its heart is the relationship between two real-life characters: the poet and soldier, Siegfried Sassoon; and a military-hospital neurologist and psychiatrist, Dr William Rivers. Sassoon has not been sent to the hospital as a victim of shell shock, but rather because of his public declaration against the continuation of the war. Pondering this clinical dilemma leads Rivers to become disillusioned; he begins to wonder whether it truly is 'madness' for soldiers to break down after facing the horrors of war or whether it is madness that so many blindly follow military orders. He eventually wonders if he himself is the mad one for 'curing' patients, only to send them back to the battlefield to be killed.

Barker herself suggests that the First World War represented 'a sort of idealism of the young people in August 1914 in Germany and in England. They really felt this was the start of a better world. And the disillusionment, the horror and the pain followed that. I think because of that it's come to stand for the pain of all wars.' Indeed, the novel delivers a powerful and eloquent but subliminal message about the folly of all wars, including those we know were to follow the 'war to end all wars'.

FROM *REGENERATION*

And as soon as you accepted that the man's breakdown was a consequence of his war experience rather than of his own innate weakness, then inevitably the war became the issue. And the therapy was a test, not only of the genuineness of the individual's symptoms, but also of the validity of the demands the war was making on him. Rivers had survived partly by suppressing his awareness of this. But then along came Sassoon and made the justifiability of the war a matter for constant, open debate, and that suppression was no longer possible. At times it seemed to Rivers that all his other patients were the anvil and that Sassoon was the hammer. Inevitably there were times when he resented this. As a civilian, Rivers's life had consisted of asking questions, and devising methods by which truthful answers could be obtained, but there are limits to how many *fundamental* questions you want to ask in a working day that starts before eight a.m. and doesn't end till midnight.

Pat Barker

EMMA CHICHESTER CLARK –
Illustrator and author

I first read *Birdsong* many years ago and remember being fascinated by the tunnelling episodes. I hadn't realized how much of the First World War had been fought underground, so when Michael asked me to contribute to this collection, I immediately thought of it.

When I found the book, it fell open on these pages – an incident I'd completely forgotten where a small mishap follows a catastrophe. It's just a little story within a vast one, but it involves every human feeling and illuminates the paradoxical nature of war.

From *Birdsong*

Weir was in the trench when the explosion went off, drinking tea with Stephen and explaining his difficulties. He went white as the earth rocked under them. The hot liquid spilled unremarked over his shaking hand.

'I knew it,' he said. 'I knew they'd blow it. I've got to get down there. It was my idea to put them there. Oh God, I *knew* this would happen.'

He looked frantically to Stephen for sympathy, then brushed past him on his way to the tunnel ahead.

'Just a minute,' said Stephen. 'You may have lost three men

down there, but if the enemy's got a tunnel under this trench I'm going to lose half my company. You'd better be bloody sure where their tunnel's going.'

'You come and see if you're so concerned. I have to think of my own men first,' said Weir.

'Take one of your men and get him to report back to me.'

Weir was so angry that he had stopped trembling. 'Don't you tell me what to do. If you're so worried about your men then you—'

'Of course I'm worried about them. If they think there's a mine under them they won't stay put for twenty-four hours. There'll be a mutiny.'

'Well, come down and bloody well see for yourself then.'

'It's not my job to crawl around underground.'

Stephen was following Weir along the trench to where he kept the tunnelling supplies. He picked up a canary in a small wooden cage and turned to face Stephen.

'Are you frightened?' said Weir.

Stephen hesitated, glancing at the cage. 'Of course not. I merely—'

'Well, come on then.'

Stephen, who had not often felt himself out-argued by Weir, saw that he had little choice.

'It'll only take an hour,' said Weir, more placatingly now that he could see Stephen weakening. There was a pause. 'You got wounded last time, didn't you? So now I suppose you're afraid to go down.'

'No,' said Stephen, 'I'm not frightened of going underground.'

Weir passed him a helmet with a lamp on it and a pick. 'It's very narrow there, and we'll need to clear some debris when we get to the explosion.'

Stephen nodded silently. He instructed the nearest man he could see to tell Ellis where he had gone, then followed Weir to the head of the tunnel.

A piece of tarpaulin was stretched over a wooden frame built back only a couple of feet from the front wall of the trench. The excavated clay was taken away in sandbags and dumped well to the rear so that enemy planes could have no idea where the digging was being done. The opening was not much more than a rabbit hole.

Weir turned to Stephen, his face set in anxiety. 'Follow me as fast as you can.'

Beneath the parapet of the trench was a vertical shaft into the darkness of the earth. The horizontal wooden rungs were several feet apart. Weir scrambled down with practised ease holding the handle of the canary's cage in his teeth, but Stephen had to feel ahead for each slat of wood with his feet.

Eventually he reached a wooden platform where Weir was waiting.

'Come on, for God's sake. This is it. It's only a shallow tunnel.'

Stephen, breathing hard, said, 'Shouldn't you have sent the stretcher-bearers?'

'Yes, they're ready, but they won't come unless an officer has told them where to go.'

Weir went forward at a crouch into the darkness, carrying the cage in his left hand. Stephen followed three or four paces behind. The bird was chirping, though whether from fear or happiness he could not say. Stephen shuddered at the sound. He thought of the surface of the earth above them: a pattern of round shellholes that made up no man's land, each one half-filled with water, in which the rats played and feasted on the unrescued corpses; then thirty feet or so of packed, resistant clay, down which the moisture could still permeate from the world above them.

Weir had gone on to his hands and knees as the height of the tunnel decreased to about three feet. The sides of it pressed in on them and Stephen found it hard to see the beam of Weir's lamp ahead of him. His own seemed to illuminate only the nails on the soles of Weir's boots and the occasional glimpse of cloth on his slowly advancing rear.

As they went further, Stephen felt the clay stick to his crawling hands. He wanted to put out his arms to his sides and push back the flanks of the tunnel to give them space to breathe. As long as Weir's body was between him and the cage, however, any fear he felt from the enclosing weight of the earth was tolerable. Anything was bearable provided he did not have to come too close to that bird.

Weir's breath was coming in fast, loud gasps as he pushed onwards, using one hand to pull himself and one to drag the cage. Stephen felt a piece of rock slit the skin of his left hand. There was nothing he could do. The earth above them was poisoned by the spores of gas gangrene, a horse disease implanted by the copious manure used by farmers; he hoped it had not sunk so deep below the surface. He pressed on, trying to put his weight on the outside of his hand. The tunnel was now so narrow that they had to try to enlarge it with their picks. There was no room to bring sufficient leverage, however, so their progress was very slow.

Weir suddenly stopped, and Stephen heard him swearing.

'This is it,' he said. 'This is the end. There should be another thirty feet. They've blown the whole bloody thing. They'll both be dead.'

Stephen came up and saw the wall of earth in front of them. He felt a sudden panic. If the tunnel behind them should also now collapse . . . He moved his feet reflexively and began to manoeuvre to turn round: such an explosion must surely have weakened the whole structure with its flimsy supporting timbers.

From his haversack Weir took a round wooden disc which he pressed against the side of the tunnel. Then he took out a stethoscope and plugged it into a teat on the surface of the disc and listened. He raised his finger to his lips. Stephen had no intention of interrupting. He listened carefully himself. It was curiously quiet. There was something unsettling about the silence: there were no guns.

Weir tore the stethoscope from his ears. 'Nothing,' he said.

'Is that thing effective?'

'Yes, it's good. A scientist in Paris invented it. You can never be sure, of course.'

'Who was in there?'

'Shaw was one. The other was called Stanley, I think. He was new.'

'And how do we get them out?'

'We don't. If we try to dig out this stuff we'll just bring in the roof. We send down some men to timber it, and if they can get through, so much the better. But I want to close this tunnel now.'

'And if they don't get to them?'

'We say a prayer. We're all buried in the end.'

'Do you want to say a prayer now?'

Weir's face was so close to his that Stephen could smell the stale alcohol on his breath. 'I don't know any prayers,' he said. 'Do you?'

'I could invent one.' The canary let out a small living

sound. Stephen ached with fear. Words came from his lips. 'Into your hand, oh God, we commend the souls of these two men. May they rest in peace. Let this not be in vain. In Jesus Christ's name. Amen.'

'Let's go,' said Weir. 'You'd better let me lead the way. I'll try and get past you. Move back a bit that way, that's it, push up against the wall.'

Stephen flattened himself to try to let Weir pass over him. As Weir's body pressed against him his trailing pick caught against the clay above. A lump of it fell on him. The space dislodged a much heavier fall which smashed down on to his right arm. He let out a cry. Stephen instinctively tried to pull back to where the tunnel was wider in case the whole thing collapsed. Weir was swearing and groaning.

'My arm's broken. Get me out, get me out. Quick or the whole thing's going to come down.'

Stephen went back to him and began to lift the fallen earth very carefully off his body. He pushed it back towards the face of the blocked tunnel. Weir was moaning in pain.

'Get it off, get it off. We've got to get out.'

Stephen, through grinding teeth, said, 'I'm doing my best. I've got to be gentle.' He was lying on top of Weir, his head towards Weir's feet, as he cleared the debris from his arm. He then had to wriggle back over Weir's body, forcing his face down into the earth with his weight. He finally got back so they were lying face to face, Weir's feet towards the wall, Stephen's towards the way out. Weir spluttered on the clay in his mouth.

'Can you make it?' said Stephen.

'I've broken my arm. Maybe a rib too. I'll have to crawl on one hand. You take the bird.'

Stephen reached back to the cage. Its flimsy wooden frame

had been crushed in the fall of the earth; it was empty.

'The bird's gone,' he said. 'Let's go.'

'Damnation,' said Weir. 'We can't leave it. We'll have to find it and take it back. Otherwise if the Boche find it they'll know we—'

'For Christ's sake, they know there's a tunnel anyway. That's why they blew it.'

Weir spat through his pain. 'You cannot under any circumstances leave a bird free. Ever. It's in the handbook. I'd be court-martialled. Find the bird.'

Stephen crawled back over Weir's prostrate body. He felt himself close to tears as he searched the murk of the clay with the feeble light of his helmet. A little to the left of the hole made by the fall he saw a gleam of yellow. Gently, he reached out his hands towards it.

He could feel his heart pummelling the floor of the tunnel; his clothes were sodden with sweat. It ran down into his eyes. He held his hand steady, the fingers opening in the gloom as he moved towards the bird. Please God, he muttered, please, please . . . When his hand was no more than six inches from the canary he made a lunge for it. The bird took off and its wings brushed the back of his hand as it flew past him. Stephen screamed. His body convulsed and his legs kicked back into Weir's thighs.

'For Christ's sake! What's the matter? You're going to bring the tunnel down.'

Stephen lay face down, panting, with his eyes closed.

'Keep still,' said Weir. 'For God's sake keep still. It's up near me now.'

Stephen lay quietly, saying nothing. Weir made no movement. Stephen heard him make little whistling noises.

He was trying to soothe the startled bird, or trick it into his hand. Stephen was still facing the wrong way. Weir's body was blocking his exit back to the light.

He felt Weir make a sudden movement. 'I've got it,' he said. 'It's in my hand.'

'All right. Let's go. You start off and I'll follow.'

'I've only got one hand. I can't take the bird.'

'Well, kill it. It's only a canary. Come on. I want to turn round. I'm getting cramp. I want to get out of here.'

There was a silence. Weir made no movement. Eventually he said, 'I can't kill it. I can't do it.'

Stephen felt a strange weight in his stomach. 'You must kill it,' he said. His voice came softly through his dry mouth.

There was another silence. Then Weir said, 'I can't do it, Wraysford. I can't do it. It's just a tiny bird. It's done nothing wrong.'

Stephen, trying to keep control over himself, said, 'For God's sake kill it. Just squeeze it in your hand. Bite its head. Anything.'

'You do it.'

'No! It's too risky passing it back to me. It might escape.'

Weir rolled over on to his back and held his left fist towards Stephen. The bird's head appeared between the forefinger and thumb. 'There it is,' Weir said. 'I'll hold it still while you take your knife and just cut its throat.'

Stephen felt Weir's eyes boring into him. He reached into his pocket and found his knife. He opened the blade and reached up over Weir's knees. Weir, straining up on his back, was able to meet his gaze as Stephen's head appeared between his shins. The two men looked at each other over the tiny yellow head between them. Stephen thought of the lines of men he had seen walking into the guns; he thought of the world screaming in the twilight at Thiepval. Weir looked steadily at him. Stephen put the knife away in his pocket. He fought back the rising tears. Weir might let the bird go. It might touch him.

'I'll take it,' he said.

'You'll need both hands to dig and crawl,' said Weir.

'I know.'

With his handkerchief Stephen made a sling for the bird. He tied three corners together and left an opening.

'All right. Put it in there and I'll tie it up.'

With teeth clamped very tight together he held out both hands to Weir, who released the bird into the handkerchief. Stephen jumped as he felt the battering of wings against the palms of his hands. He managed with fumbling fingers to bring the fourth corner of the handkerchief into the other three and tie it. He put the knot between his teeth and crawled back over Weir's body.

They began their slow retreat, Stephen pushing back the loose earth and enlarging the tunnel where he could. Weir fought his way with his left hand.

In the narrow darkness Stephen felt the feathery weight beneath his face. Sometimes the bird beat its wings and struggled, sometimes it lay still in fear. He saw in his mind the stretched skeleton of the lower wing, the darting movement of the head, and the black, relentless eyes. He tried to turn his mind away from it by thinking of other things, but no other thought would lodge in his mind. It was as though his brain had closed down, leaving only one picture: the fossil shape of a bird, a pterodactyl ribbed in limestone, the long cruel beak with its prehistoric hook and the bones fanned out, their exiguous width and enormous span, particularly the underside of the breakable wing, with its sinewy feathers plugged into the bird's blood at one end, then stretched over the delta that would flap and bang in his face as the frantic creature, in the storm of its true hostility, would bring its vast plucking beak into his eyes.

The small canary suspended from his mouth made feeble movements and its yellow feathers protruded from the handkerchief to brush softly against his face. He closed his eyes and pushed onwards. He longed for the mud and the stench, for the sound of shells.

Behind him, Weir crawled as best he could. He asked Stephen to stop as he tucked his arm into the front of his shirt for support. He shouted in pain as the two bones momentarily rubbed together.

They reached the ladder and were able to stand up. Stephen took the handkerchief from his mouth and handed it to Weir.

'I'll climb up and send a couple of your men down to help you. You hold on to this.'

Weir nodded. He was very pale, Stephen noticed. Then Weir gave the wide, empty-eyed grin that worried Ellis so much. He said, 'You're a brave man, Wraysford.'

Sebastian Faulks

CHARLIE HIGSON –
Actor, comedian and author

I've always loved comics, and have never seen them as second class to novels. I grew up with the little Commando war comics, which were read by all boys and had an enthusiastically macho attitude towards warfare and heroism. *Charley's War*, written by Pat Mills and illustrated by Joe Colquhoun, was something different. It originally appeared in *Battle Picture Weekly*, a fairly gung-ho boys' comic, and most of the other stories were of the old school 'Take that, Fritz!' variety. True, there's enough action, drama and everyday heroism in *Charley's War* to keep the average boy happy, but like all the best comics it slipped some powerful messages in under the radar, and was firmly anti-war.

Largely set in the trenches, it follows the adventures of young Charley Bourne, who lies about his age and joins the British army aged sixteen, only to find himself thrown into the brutality and misery of the Somme. The comic was different to other comics in that it didn't glorify war or flinch from the reality and horror of it. It was very well researched, with most of the stories inspired by real-life events, but it also had a much wider emotional range than other comics of the time. As a reader, you go through all the hopes and heartaches and loss that Charley and his mates go through, and the comic manages (as shown in the pages reproduced here) to be very moving. Pat Mills was also interested in the politics of war and was obviously furious at the way the lower ranks were often treated.

I wonder how many boys of Charley's age reading it in the mercifully peaceful England of the late seventies and early eighties imagined what it would have been like to be up to their knees in mud fighting a pointless war and seeing their friends killed all around them.

JEREMY IRVINE – Actor

I've always been fascinated by the pilots of the First World War. I grew up near an airfield, and would often see old biplanes in the sky above my garden. It's strange to think that these slow-moving, fragile 'kites', as they were called at the time, made of nothing more than canvas and wood, were fitted with machine guns and designed to fight and destroy one another. In the stories I read growing up, there was something quite romantic and medieval about the idea, a form of jousting in the sky; gentleman against gentleman, and a chivalry that couldn't be found in the bloody slaughter of trench warfare on the ground.

The reality, of course, could not be further from the truth. The famous nickname 'The Twenty Minuters' to describe members of the Royal Flying Corps came from the life expectancy of its pilots in the air. At the height of the war, it was just seventeen minutes before a new pilot, many of them just young boys fresh from school, could expect to be killed. Their deaths occurred in circumstances every bit as unglamorous as those of their comrades on the ground, most likely without warning, being burned alive in their cockpits with no parachute or hope of escape.

I came across the story of Albert Ball when I was nineteen, while researching for my role in the movie *War Horse*. I found it incomprehensible that by my age, only just out of school, Albert was already a combat veteran and a seasoned killer. His success as a fighter pilot and his boyish good looks would make him a nationwide celebrity and a 'pin-up' at a time when Britain was desperate for any symbol of hope to latch onto. Yet, like so many of his comrades, he would not see twenty-one.

Like me, Albert had developed a passion for flying while growing up; in fact, we both learned to fly at the same aerodrome at RAF Hendon, although I was still at school with the cadets, and Albert was preparing for his first posting to a combat squadron in France. Flying itself was still a very new invention, and at the beginning of the war more pilots were killed in training than in actual combat – as Albert said in a letter home to his mother:

Well my flying is going fine, but I'm very sorry to say a great many of our men have been killed the last few weeks ... Yesterday a ripping boy had a smash and when we got to him he had a two inch piece of wood right through his head ...

Followed by:

If you would like a flight I should be so pleased to take you up any time you wish.

Two weeks after being given his 'wings', Albert was posted to France. Unbeknown to him, he had arrived during one of the darkest hours for the RFC, yet he survived his first months, and his aggressiveness quickly led to him becoming an established fighter pilot with an increasing number of 'kills'. Stories of his successes soon began to spread and the British press began to take notice of this new 'hero of the air'. However, his letters home and the memoirs of officers who knew him show a much darker side. His younger brother, Cyril, eager to follow in his brother's footsteps, had expressed an interest in joining the RFC. In a letter home Albert pleads:

> Please tell Cyril that perhaps he had better stick to his regiment. I like this job, but nerves do not last long, and you soon want a rest ... I can stand a lot but it is beginning to tell on me. I always feel tired ... Do please ask him to keep out of the RFC. I shall send him a long letter the first chance I get, in fact I will start tonight.

I find this incredibly moving – perhaps because I too have younger brothers, but also because of his apparent resignation to his fate. He goes on to say:

> Re – you saying that if anything happens to me ... if anything did happen, as it quite easily may, I expect and wish you to take it well, for men tons better than me go in hundreds every day.

Like most airmen of the First World War, Albert understood that it was only a matter of time before he too fell victim. Mick Manock, another fighter ace, was once asked what he intended to do after the war. He simply replied that there would be no 'after the war' for a fighter pilot.

As the weeks went by, the constant strain began to tell on Albert. This was before the effects of post-traumatic stress were understood, and reading his letters, you can see Albert beginning to show some very odd behaviour. There is a photo of him building what looks like a makeshift garden shed. In fact, Albert had decided that instead of living in billets with the other pilots, he would build and live in a hut next to his aeroplane, preferring to live in solitude and in a constant state of readiness. This solitude was not just limited to his time on the ground; Albert refused to fly with wingmen, preferring 'lone wolf' missions. There are accounts of him circling over German airfields, goading the enemy fighters to come up to meet him. On one occasion, twelve enemy aircraft came up to ward off the lone fighter, but Albert was undeterred by numerical odds. In the battle that followed, his ignition leads were slashed by enemy fire and his engine seized; refusing to surrender, he kept firing until his guns went silent. With a dead engine and no ammunition, Albert pulled out his Colt automatic pistol and, in his frustration, emptied a full clip at his opponents. After a similar escapade, the recording officer describes Albert's return to the squadron.

Flushed in the face, his eyes brilliant, his hair blown and dishevelled, he came into the squadron office to make his report, but for a long time was in so over wrought a state, that dictation was an impossibility to him. 'God is very good to me.' 'God must have me in His keeping' was all he could say.

It's easy to forget that Albert was still only twenty years old. Knowing that his nerves were on the brink of snapping and in desperate need of rest, he requested leave to go home. The leave was granted, but it was far from the rest he so desperately needed.

Albert's success had come at a time when the British public were still reeling from the losses on the Somme. The British government needed a distraction, a symbol of hope they could exploit to raise morale on the Home Front. Unwittingly, Albert had become that symbol: a whirlwind of photographers and newspaper journalists greeted him at his front door. He found he couldn't walk down the street without people stopping him, and soon took to wearing his civilian clothes to try and reclaim some anonymity. His 'restful' leave was filled with a blur of formal events, including one at Buckingham Palace to receive his Military Cross and DSO. Reading his letters, I believe it was this exploitation when home on leave that finally pushed Albert over the edge. During one event he is said to have whispered to his father, 'I'd sooner face a Hun in the air than all this.'

Albert secured a posting back to France, but he appeared to know that he would be leaving for the last time. During his last visit home, he slipped quietly up to his room, carefully wrapped all his belongings and private papers, and left them in neat piles. Finally, he left a note to his mother with instructions on how his personal affairs should be handled.

Deprived of his rest, Albert arrived back in France. He is said to have complained to his CO that he was 'Taking unnecessary risks of late.' One diary entry simply says:

> Dud day. Went on patrol and saw nothing. At night, cleared up, so went up and attacked 20 Huns. Arrived back at dark with all ammunition used up.

At the time Albert had a total of thirty-eight victories, and his CO agreed that when he reached forty he would be granted another period's leave. He explains as much that night in the last letter he would ever write to his father. He finishes with:

> I do get tired of always living to kill, and am really beginning to feel like a murderer. Shall be so pleased when I have finished.

I find these last lines particularly poignant. Perhaps I read too much into them, but I like to think that they show some premonition.

Albert would be killed the following day.

He reached his total of forty kills on the morning of 7 May 1917. Due to leave for home in a matter of days, he tended the small garden he had dug next to his hut before taking off with the rest of his flight for a scheduled photographic reconnaissance mission. Unknown to Albert, in his absence, the squadron major was busy putting together Albert's recommendation for a Victoria Cross.

Crossing the German lines, the squadron soon ran into enemy planes, and Albert became locked in a dogfight with a particularly skilled German pilot. Little did he know that the enemy squadron was that of the famous Red Baron, Manfred von Richthofen, and the pilot he was facing was the Baron's own brother, Lothar von

Richthofen. In the fight that followed, one of Albert's bullets pierced Lothar's fuel tank and he was forced to make an emergency landing in a field below. Albert's squadron-mate Cecil Crowe then watched as Albert zoomed up, victorious, into a dark thundercloud before appearing again seconds later, upside-down, with a dead prop; he crashed into the ground below.

A local farm girl, Mademoiselle Cécile Deloffre, was the first on the scene. She lifted him, unconscious but still breathing, out of the broken wreckage of his machine, and held him. Albert lived only a few minutes, opening his eyes just once.

Richthofen was credited with shooting Albert down, but to this day the real reasons for his death are unknown. On inspection, there was no damage to himself or his machine from enemy fire, and with Ball's experience it's hard to believe it was pilot error. After the war his grief-stricken father, desperate for answers, travelled to interview a Belgian nurse who had worked in the field hospital where Albert's body had been taken. She told him that Albert had died from a heart attack just prior to crashing into the ground. Albert's father chose to believe her, and subsequently refused to hear any other explanation.

The Germans, who dubbed Albert 'the English Richthofen', gave him a funeral with full military honours, a rare sign of respect at this stage in the war. Over the grave they inscribed the words:

FALLEN IN AIR COMBAT FOR HIS FATHERLAND
ENGLISH PILOT CAPTAIN ALBERT BALL

Back home in England, a memorial service was held for the fallen hero and Albert was posthumously awarded the VC. Large crowds lined the streets of his native Nottingham, yet his mother, overcome with grief, could not face attending. A fellow pilot who flew with him on his last flight commented, 'I see they have given him the VC. Of course he won it a dozen times over – the whole squadron knows that.'

His parents left his room exactly as it was for ten years, just in case.

BEN ELTON – Comedian, author, actor and director

From the time of its first publication in 1929, *All Quiet on the Western Front* has been described as an 'anti-war novel'. But all its author, Erich Maria Remarque, ever hoped to do was give a true picture of the experiences of an ordinary soldier in the trenches. He does this so well, and those experiences were so appalling, that the result could scarcely be seen as anything other than 'anti' war.

But it's not all grim. The book is also a wonderfully human story filled with warm, compelling characters and vividly descriptive passages showing not just the horror of life at the front but also its tender, and even funny, side. I read the book in my teens, and forty years later still recall the brilliant scene where Remarque describes the curious peace and comradely conviviality of a platoon communal smoke and crap.

Apart from life in the trenches, the other principal theme of the book is how alien soldiers felt when on leave, and how impossible they found it to convey anything of what they were going through to the people back home. This is a very common theme of Great War writing. All the sabre-rattling and jingoism took place amongst civilians and armchair warriors; there was almost none of it at the front.

All Quiet on the Western Front is a German book, and perhaps I feel drawn to it because one of my grandfathers was a German soldier from 1914 to 1918; he even won an Iron Cross (third class)! His story is a good illustration of the irony and futility of war because, as a Jew, this decorated German veteran was later forced to flee Nazi Germany. He was lucky; many of his relatives were murdered.

Perhaps the best recommendation of all I can make for *All Quiet on the Western Front* is that the Nazis hated it. It was one of the first books they banned and publicly burned after seizing power. Read it for that reason alone!

PREFACE TO *ALL QUIET ON THE WESTERN FRONT*

This book is to be neither an accusation nor a confession, and least of all an adventure, for death is not an adventure to those who stand face to face with it. It will try simply to tell of a generation of men who, even though they may have escaped shells, were destroyed by the war.

Erich Maria Remarque

CAROLINE WYATT – Journalist

All Quiet on the Western Front is a book that I first read when I was seventeen, just a little bit younger than the novel's narrator, Paul. I was studying German at school, and living in West Berlin at the time, and it helped me understand the First World War from a German soldier's point of view.

It was also the book that I took with me when, many years later, in 2007, I went to Helmand in Afghanistan as a reporter, to embed with British troops that Christmas. I read it while staying at a cold forward operating base with my BBC cameraman, Chris Parkinson. We were filming with British forces who were the same age as Paul, and who were daily going out on patrol, even on Christmas Day, in hostile territory, doubtless feeling some of the same sort of fear, yet having to confront it and overcome it every single day.

Talking to the young Royal Marines and filming with them during the day, and then reading the book late at night by torchlight as I tried to get to sleep, shivering in my sleeping bag, gave the novel a whole new meaning and resonance for me, as well as proof of the timeless truths that it tells about war – any war – and the strange mixture of fear, boredom, terror – and unexpected laughter, jokes and the love of life that accompany armed conflict.

Whatever the year, and whatever the conflict, the soldiers who fight or die or are wounded will probably all feel the emotions that this young German soldier expresses in the novel – from occasional exhilaration to sheer paralysing terror. And perhaps, like Paul, soldiers today still find courage within themselves to conquer their fears – not by following orders or ideals, but thanks to their comrades.

I thought of the book again when we talked a few years later to a young infantryman, James McKie, who was awarded a medal for his bravery in Helmand. He saved the lives of several of his comrades when he picked up a hand grenade – thrown by the Taliban – which had landed on the roof they were on. He picked it up and threw it back at the insurgents seconds before it went off. When I asked him whether he'd been scared, he just said that he hadn't had time – all he could think of was making sure that his mates were all right.

In this extract, Paul has come back from leave; on his first patrol since his return, he is petrified and hides in a trench. But then he hears the voices of his comrades.

From *All Quiet on the Western Front*

I am fighting a crazy, confused battle. I want to get out of my hollow in the ground and I keep on slipping back in; I say to myself, 'You've got to, it's to do with your mates, not some stupid order,' and straight after that: 'So what? I've only got the one life to lose.'

Suddenly a surprising warmth comes over me. Those voices, those few soft words, those footsteps in the trench behind me tear me with a jolt away from the terrible feeling of isolation that goes with the fear of death, to which I nearly succumbed. Those voices mean more than my life, more than mothering and fear, they are the strongest and most protective thing that there is: they are the voices of my pals.

I'm no longer a shivering scrap of humanity alone in the dark – I belong to them and they to me, we all share the same fear and the same life, and we are bound to each other in a strong and simple way. I want to press my face into them, those voices, those few words that saved me, and which will be my support.

Erich Maria Remarque

CATHY NEWMAN – Journalist

In 1915, twenty-year-old journalist Dorothy Lawrence fulfilled her ambition to see action on the Western Front – by pretending to be a man. It was the only way she could do it.

Frustrated by her editor's refusal to employ her as a war correspondent, Lawrence travelled to Paris, where two soldiers she met in a café helped her by smuggling out items of uniform with their washing. Having darkened her skin with furniture polish and bulked out her shoulders with sacking, she made her way towards the front with faked papers identifying her as Denis Smith, 1st Battalion Leicestershire Regiment.

The plan worked well – until, quite suddenly, it didn't. Lawrence befriended a soldier called Tom Dunn, who risked court martial by smuggling her into the trenches. Lawrence worked alongside Dunn laying mines in no man's land, a few hundred yards from the German trenches. But the stress of the job triggered panic attacks and fainting fits, and after ten days she gave herself up, worried that by staying she might unwittingly endanger her colleagues.

The First World War might have been a 'total war', but in Britain at least that didn't extend to women being allowed to fight. For the most part they 'kept the home fires burning', working in munitions factories or, at the other end of the spectrum, knitting socks for soldiers. In one sense, Lawrence's story was a bit of a setback for feminism – she gave up, after all. But imagine the extra stress of having to conceal your true identity under those conditions. Without that burden, there's every reason to suppose Lawrence would have been as capable as the men – especially when you consider what women did, with the government's blessing, on the Western Front.

Which brings me to my chosen extract, from Helen Zenna Smith's brilliant, horrifying *Not So Quiet* – one of my favourite books about the war.

Helen Zenna Smith was the pen-name of a journalist called Evadne Price. Asked by a publisher to write a parody of Erich Remarque's famous 1929 novel *All Quiet on the Western Front*, Price decided she would rather write a serious work which gave an honest account of the role women had played in the Great War. (*All Quiet . . .* was, she thought, a 'wonderful book' which 'anybody would be mad to make fun of'.)

To make her novel as realistic as possible, she used as her starting point the diary of a real-life ambulance-driver in France, Winifred Constance Young. Young had wanted to publish a memoir of her experiences, but worried about embarrassing her family, who didn't want to hear about the awful things she had endured. Price turned Young's writing into a work of fiction – and it was a great success.

Published in 1930, it was a bestseller and won the Prix Séverigne as 'the novel most calculated to promote international peace'.

In 1914, women who wanted to join the services had limited options. If they were over twenty-three, they could be Voluntary Aid Detachments (VADs) – semi-trained assistant nurses, of whom there were 38,000 by the time the war ended. Otherwise they could, like the heroines of *Not So Quiet*, be FANYs: members of the First Aid Nursing Yeomanry – ambulance-drivers who ferried the wounded from the front line to field hospitals.

The extract I've chosen makes quite clear what grim work this was: 'The foulest and most disgusting job it is possible to imagine.'

And bear in mind, the 'FANYs' were usually well-to-do women who in many cases had never left the family home before. What they found in France must have shocked them to the core. The cramped, filthy conditions, awful food and lack of sleep were hard enough to bear; but add to that the sight (and sound, and smell) of dying men with unimaginably damaged bodies. But they had to simply get on with it – 'no time for squeamishness'.

Amid the horror, though, there is camaraderie. Firm friendships are made, and Price captures the off-duty moments of levity frankly and with fantastic wit.

FROM *NOT SO QUIET*

Cleaning an ambulance is the foulest and most disgusting job it is possible to imagine. We are unanimous on this point. Even yet we hardened old-timers cannot manage it without 'catting' on exceptionally bad mornings. We do not mind cleaning the engines, doing repairs and keeping the outsides presentable – it is dealing with the insides we hate.

The stench that comes out as we open the doors each morning nearly knocks us down. Pools of stale vomit from the poor wretches we have carried the night before, corners the sitters have turned into temporary lavatories for all purposes, blood and mud and vermin and the stale stench of stinking trench feet and gangrenous wounds. Poor souls, they cannot help it. No one blames them. Half the time they are unconscious of what they are doing, wracked with pain and jolted about on the rough roads, for, try as we may – and the cases all agree that women drivers are ten times more thoughtful than the men drivers – we cannot altogether evade the snow-covered stones and potholes.

How we dread the morning clean-out of the insides of our cars, we gently-bred, educated women they insist on so rigidly for this work that apparently cannot be done by women incapable of speaking English with a public-school accent!

'Our ambulance women take entire control of their cars, doing all running repairs and all cleaning.'

This appeared in a signed article by one of our head officials in London, forwarded to me by Mother last week. It was entitled 'Our Splendid Women'. I wondered then how many people comfortably reading it over the breakfast table realized what that 'all cleaning' entailed. None, I should imagine; much less the writer of the muck. Certainly we ourselves had no idea before we got there.

I wonder afresh as I don my overalls and rubber boots. I know what to expect this morning, remembering that poor wretched soul I carried on my last trek to Number Thirteen, who will be buried by one of us today.

I am nearly sick on the spot at the sight greeting me, but I have no time for squeamishness. I have Commandant's bus in addition to my own to get through.

The snow is coming down pretty heavily now, the waterproof sheet over my bonnet is full, and the red cross over the front of the driving seat totally obscured by a white pall. Blue-nosed, blue-overalled drivers in knee-high waterproof boots are diligently carrying buckets of water and getting out cloths in readiness for the great attack. The smell of disinfectant is everywhere. No one speaks much. It is a wretched morning and the less one talks the sooner one will be out of these whirling flakes.

The inside of my ambulance is at last cleared of its filth. I swill it with water. More water. Now with disinfectant. I examine it minutely. Commandant's 11 to 12 inspection is no idle formality. She goes over every square inch of each ambulance, inside and out, the engines are revved up, the tyre pressures tested, everything. With all her faults, she knows her job. If only she had a little heart, she would be an ideal woman for this sort of work. Why is it that women in authority almost invariably fall victims to megalomania?

Now for the engine. I start up after ten minutes' hard work, for the engine is stone-cold. Something is wrong. A choked carburettor? I clean it. No better. She doesn't seem to be getting the petrol quickly enough. A dirty feed? Or a plug? I test the

plugs. They are OK. It must be the petrol pipe. It is. I listen. She is running sweetly enough now.

Tyres are all right, thank heaven. Perhaps a little more air in the offside rear? Done.

Helen Zenna Smith

MEG ROSOFF – Writer

In this passage from Ford Madox Ford's *Parade's End*, our hero recounts the everyday horrors of war in a voice that is by turns poetic and matter-of-fact. Though not exactly cut out to be an officer, Tietjens finds himself at the front line trying to do the best for his men – with kindness, humour and a sort of relentless, weary patience. And we readers are right there with him, trudging through a waterlogged trench filled with icy sucking mud, severed limbs and blood – with no option but to carry on.

From *A Man Could Stand Up,* PART OF THE *Parade's End* TRILOGY

In the trench you could see nothing and noise rushed like black angels gone mad; solid noise that swept you off your feet . . . Swept your brain off its feet. Something else took control of it. You became second-in-command of your own soul. Waiting for its C.O. to be squashed flat by the direct hit of a four point two before you got control again.

There was nothing to see; mad lights whirled over the black heavens. He moved along the mud of the trench. It amazed him to find that it was raining. In torrents. You imagined that the heavenly powers in decency suspended their activities at such moments. They didn't! A Verey light or something extinguished *that* – not very efficient lightning, really. Just at that moment he fell on his nose at an angle of forty-five degrees against some squashed earth where, as he remembered, the parapet had been revetted. The trench had been squashed in, level with the outside ground. A pair of boots emerged from the pile of mud. How the deuce did the fellow get into that position?

Ford Madox Ford

HELEN SKELTON – Presenter and writer

Breakfast in our house was always a battle: my big brother picking bogeys out of his nose while I made a wall of cereal boxes between him and me. I must have thought that if he was out of sight, he'd be out of mind! Maybe I was just worried he would flick green slimy snot into my Coco Pops. Either way, it was the meal that set the tone for the day; the brother–sister bickering started at the breakfast table and didn't end until bedtime.

It was frantic and chaotic, with Mam rushing us and repeating the time minute by minute. At eight a.m., three hours into his working day, my dad would usually join us for at least one round of bogey-dodging.

By the time we reached secondary-school age it was a family tradition and the most well-rehearsed family meal we had, although we didn't know it at the time. It was a meal we took for granted, one we always knew would be laid out on the table, one so reliable and consistent that we could put on a side show around it.

Breakfast since then always has and always will be my favourite meal of the day.

For me breakfast signals a new day and therefore a fresh start. Not for the soldiers speaking in Gibson's poem. As it was for me, breakfast for them was a daily ritual; they describe it as one of those things you just do, apparently uninterrupted despite the imminent threat of death from overhead bullets. To me, the poem is an amazing example of how those soldiers just 'got on with it'. They adapted their lives and routines to the crazy situation they were in. The reference to football, and jokes over who will win pending matches immediately stirs memories of school-bus conversations I overheard. In this poem they don't seem like soliders fighting war and chalking up deaths with pride. They are lads, talking football over breakfast, which makes what happens next all the more shocking.

BREAKFAST

We ate our breakfast lying on our backs,
Because the shells were screeching overhead.
I bet a rasher to a loaf of bread
That Hull United would beat Halifax
When Jimmy Stainthorp played full-back instead
Of Billy Bradford. Ginger raised his head
And cursed, and took the bet; and dropt back dead.
We ate our breakfast lying on our backs,
Because the shells were screeching overhead.

Wilfrid Wilson Gibson

SUSAN COOPER – Author

My dad fought in the First World War when he was eighteen. He was lucky; he was wounded and sent home, instead of being killed like my uncle and almost a million other young Englishmen. He talked about life in the trenches only once, and you wouldn't want to hear what he said.

The writer-artist David Jones was in the trenches too, at the same age. His astonishing prose poem *In Parenthesis* tells about it, through his own eyes and those of soldiers back through the ages. Painting with words and punctuation, scoring them like music, he gives a grindingly vivid picture of the daily life of men in that terrible war. And reminds us that all war is terrible.

FROM *IN PARENTHESIS*

They fell in after dark, greatcoats folded outside packs, and after the first mile you got uncomfortably hot under the rubber sheeting and with the halt you cooled and shivered; people didn't talk much, and there was little sound at all, but what the weather made, when the feet marching, shuffled to a standstill. The gunfire from the south-east had become for them so normal an accompaniment as to be no longer noted, its cadences unheeded; but at the second halt you began to enquire of this new stillness on the night. Perhaps it was because of the lie of the land, or perhaps he'd beat it right out of hearing, or perhaps this lull were a space between, a breather for them. At all events, the wind bore no sound, other than itself, across the drenched land; or if that changing light as on each other night, danced, for a gunned piping, this hill's bulk kept you uncertain.

But soon, you only but half-heard words of command, and your body conformed to those bodies about, and you slept upright, where these marched, because of the balm of this shower, of the darkness, of the measure of the beat of feet in unison . . .

* * *

It was largely his machine guns in Acid Copse that did it, and our own heavies firing by map reference, with all lines phut and no reliable liaison.

So you just lay where you were and shielded what you could of your body.

It slackened a little and they try short rushes and you find yourself alone in a denseness of hazel-brush and body high bramble and between the bright interstices and multifarious green-stuff, grey textile, scarlet-edged goes and comes – and there is another withdrawing-heel from the thicket.

His light stick-bomb winged above your thorn-bush, and aged oak-timbers shiver and leaves shower like thrown blossom for a conqueror.

You tug at rusted pin —

it gives unexpectedly and your fingers pressed to release flange.

You loose the thing into the underbrush.

Dark-faceted iron oval lobs heavily to fungus-cushioned dank, wobbles under low leaf to lie, near where the heel drew out just now; and tough root-fibres boomerang to top-most green filigree and earth clods flung disturb fresh fragile shoots that brush the sky.

You huddle closer to your mossy bed
you make yourself scarce
you scramble forward and pretend not to see,
but ruby drops from young beech-sprigs —
are bright your hands and face.
And the other one cries from the breaking-buckthorn.
He calls for Elsa, for Manuela
for the parish priest of Burkersdorf in Saxe Altenburg.

You grab his dropt stick-bomb as you go, but somehow you don't fancy it and anyway you forget how it works. You definitely like the coloured label on the handle, you throw it to the tall wood-weeds.

So double detonations, back and fro like well-played-up-to-service at a net, mark left and right the forcing of the groves.

But there where a small pathway winds and sun shafts play, a dozen of them walk toward, they come in file, their lifted arms like Jansenist Redeemers, who would save, at least, themselves. Some come furtively who peer sideways, inquisitive of their captors, and one hides a face twisted for intolerable pain and one other casts about him, acutely, as who would take his opportunity, but for the most part they come as sleepwalkers whose bodies go unbidden of the mind, without malevolence, seeking only rest . . .

David Jones

ANTONY BEEVOR – Historian

Perhaps more than any other period in history, the subject of the First World War has become deeply divided. On one side a popular impression of events has built up, partly influenced by *Oh! What a Lovely War*, *Blackadder* and *War Horse*. This version of a totally futile and unnecessary war concentrates on the fate of the individual, with death and squalor in the trenches, the terrible moonscape of no man's land, 'going over the top', the war poets, the executions of deserters, and the incompetence of generals mounting doomed attacks.

Most professional historians, on the other hand, while they do not in any way deny the massive tragedy and the suffering, see the war and its origins from a rather different angle.

Once the chain reaction of ultimatum and mobilization had started after the shooting in Sarajevo with the Austro-Hungarian Empire and Russia, the network of alliances which had been created to prevent war only widened the conflagration. Britain, the last to join, simply could not stay out of the conflict: her traditional strategy since the eighteenth century had always been to prevent a single power from dominating the continent of Europe.

What the popular version of the First World War overlooks is the fact that the small professional British Army which went to war in 1914 was extremely effective, and fought well to prevent a lightning German victory. But the war of movement rapidly changed to a static war of attrition, because both sides had failed to see that the invention of barbed wire and machine guns had swung the advantage overwhelmingly against the attacker. And yet political and economic pressures in Britain, in France, in Germany, in Russia, in the Austro-Hungarian Empire and in the Ottoman Empire demanded victory as soon as possible. This is where the tragedy developed. And it was doomed to continue until either one side or the other could invent new weapons to break the stranglehold of the defence, or collapse from moral or economic exhaustion.

The Kitchener armies assembled in 1915 were a sacrificial stopgap in a war of mass mobilization. Unlike the continental powers, with their conscripted armies and vast trained reserves, Britain in peacetime had maintained only a small army of volunteers. Hard lessons had to be learned. By 1918 the British Army had become a far more professional organization than its peacetime predecessor. Its victory in August 1918 during Field Marshal Haig's great counterattack, following the massive Ludendorff offensive, has often been overlooked. It was deliberately ignored later by Nazi propagandists when they claimed that the German Army had never been defeated in the field, only stabbed in the back by Jews and socialists.

> **Kitchener armies were all-volunteer armies, created by Horatio Kitchener, Secretary of State for War.**

Here are some excerpts written in August 1918 by my grandfather-in-law, Duff Cooper, a young lieutenant in the Grenadier Guards who won the Distinguished Service Order, the next decoration to a Victoria Cross. Later, he was the only senior minister to resign from the government in protest over Neville Chamberlain's Munich agreement.

The second day we remained where we were in boiling sun under heavy shellfire suffering from thirst. I have been thirsty all my life but never quite so thirsty as that. We thought to be relieved that night and lived on the hope. But as night came on we learned first that we were not to be relieved and then that we were to make another attack at four a.m. My platoon of thirty was then reduced to ten — and at the last minute as we were forming up for the attack I discovered that my sergeant was blind drunk — a dreadful moment. But it was followed by some of the most glorious of my life. A full moon, a star to guide us — a long line of cheering men, an artillery barrage as beautiful as any fireworks creeping on before us — a feeling of wild and savage joy. It is a picture that will hang in my gallery for ever, and will come next in value to three or four dozen in which you figure. The whole battalion won their objective under the scheduled time. I was the first of my Company in the German trench. I boast like a Gascon, but it was what the old war poets said war was and what the new poets say it isn't.

Letter to his fiancée, Lady Diana Manners,
25 August 1918, BEF France

In fact Duff, an inveterate gambler, could have boasted a great deal more about his next encounter with the enemy for which he won his medal, but he ascribed it to pure luck.

To tell truth my success was very largely due to the favours of that fickle goddess whose smiles I have so often courted at the green table where she so often withheld them, biding her time for this even more valuable occasion.

A detailed account appeared in his diary dated 20 August.

(Major) Fryer told me to take a Lewis gun and a couple of sections and capture or knock out the (German) machine gun. It was rather an alarming thing to be told to do. However I got my Lewis gun up to within about 80 yards of it. The Lewis gun fired away. When it stopped I rushed forward. Looking back I saw that I was not being followed. I learnt afterwards that the first two men behind me had been wounded and the third killed. The rest had not come on. One or two machine guns from the other side of the railway were firing at us. I dropped a few yards away from the gun I was going for and crawled right up to it. Looking down I saw one man running away. I had a shot at him with my revolver. Presently I saw two men moving cautiously below me. I called to them in what German I could at the moment remember to surrender and throw up their hands. They did so immediately. They obviously did not realize that I was alone. They came up with their hands up — followed to my surprise by others. There were 18 or 19 in all. If they had rushed me they would have been perfectly safe for I can never hit a haystack with a revolver and my own men were 80 yards away.

Morale in the British Army soared during these successes, and by late September German soldiers were surrendering in droves. The Nazi 'stab-in-the-back' legend could not have been more dishonest.

RICHARD CURTIS – Writer

When Ben Elton and I decided to write a situation comedy, full of stupid jokes, about the First World War, we knew it was quite an odd thing to do – to try to be funny about this epic human tragedy. But we did a little research, and found out that there had been quite a lot of comedy in the situation, the very first time that Englishmen of all classes found themselves living so close to each other – and also lots of black comedy in the stupidity of the war. But from the very start, we agreed that it had to end badly. That it had to end in sorrow. That everyone had to die. Had anyone said that they wanted a happy ending, we wouldn't have written anything at all. And so these are the very final pages of the show – when Blackadder has done everything he can to get out alive, but is finally going to have to go over the top. I have been told that over ninety per cent of all letters ever written to us about the show have been about the effect of these final two minutes.

From *BLACKADDER GOES FORTH*: 'Goodbyeee'

```
DARLING: I say, listen - our guns have stopped.
GEORGE: You don't think . . .
BALDRICK: Perhaps the war's over. Perhaps it's
peace!
GEORGE: Hurrah! The big nobs have got round a
table and yanked the iron out of the fire.
```

DARLING: Thank God. We lived through it — The
Great War, 1914-1917.

ALL THREE: Hip hip hurray!

BLACKADDER: I'm afraid not. The guns have
stopped because we are about to attack. Not
even our generals are mad enough to shell their
own men. They feel it's far more sporting to
let the Germans do it.

GEORGE: So, we are, in fact, going over. This
is, as they say, 'it'?

BLACKADDER: Yes, unless I can think of
something very quickly.

A command is heard: 'Company, one pace
forward.' They all take one step forward.

BALDRICK: There's a nasty splinter on that
ladder, sir. A bloke could hurt himself on
that.

A call: 'Stand ready.' They put their hands on
the ladders, ready to climb over.

BALDRICK: I have a plan, sir.

BLACKADDER: Really, Baldrick, a cunning and
subtle one?

BALDRICK: Yes, sir.

BLACKADDER: As cunning as a fox who's just
been appointed Professor of Cunning at Oxford
University?

BALDRICK: Yes, sir.

Another call is heard: 'On the signal', Company
will advance!'

BLACKADDER: Well I'm afraid it's too late.
Whatever it was, I'm sure it was better than

Captain Edmund Blackadder and Private S. Baldrick

my plan to get out of this by pretending to be
mad. I mean, who would have noticed another
madman round here?

A whistle goes. He looks at Baldrick.

BLACKADDER: Good luck, everyone.

Blackadder blows his whistle. There is a roar
of voices — everyone leaps up the ladders. As
they rise above the sandbags they are met by
thunderous machine-gun fire.

Blackadder, Baldrick, George and Darling run
on, brandishing their handguns. They will not
get far.

Silence falls. Our soldiers fade away. No
Man's Land turns slowly into a peaceful field
of poppies. The only sound is that of a bird,
singing sweetly.

ANTHONY HOROWITZ – Author

There were many great poets of the First World War and you'll find them well represented in this book. However, I've chosen a song that has no known author. It seems to have sprung up from nowhere and was sung in the trenches by ordinary soldiers who had to deal with the horrors of modern warfare. Mustard gas would actually burn the flesh off their bones – it was a vile weapon – but here it's treated with very dark humour. That seems to me to be quite extraordinarily courageous in itself.

If you get a chance, see Richard Attenborough's brilliant anti-war film, *Oh! What a Lovely War*, which uses many of these songs. They need to be heard rather than read. They are echoes of history, as potent now as they were then, and one can only hope we never have to hear them again.

 ## BOMBED LAST NIGHT

Bombed last night and bombed the night before
Going to get bombed tonight if we never get bombed anymore.
When we're bombed, we're scared as we can be.
Can't stop the bombing from old Higher Germany.

They're warning us, they're warning us.
One shell hole for just the four of us
Thank your lucky stars there are no more of us.
'Cos one of us can fill it all alone.

Gassed last night and gassed the night before
Going to get gassed tonight if we never get gassed anymore.
When we're gassed we're sick as we can be.
For Phosgene and Mustard Gas is much too much for me.

They're killing us, they're killing us.
One respirator for the four of us.
Thank your lucky stars there is no more of us.
So one of us can take it all alone.

Anon.

DAVID ALMOND – Author

Oh, What a Lovely War! is a variety show, a series of songs and sketches and jokes. It's an exuberant and compelling recreation of early-twentieth-century music hall. Rooted in the culture of everyman, it speaks in a common tongue, is a work of art for everyone, and is terrifying and profound. It speaks of the First World War, and is beautifully specific in its references to named generals and rulers, battles and casualty numbers, in its speech patterns and its songs. But it is about all wars.

I saw it first as a movie in 1970, when the Vietnam War was still raging, and when we all lived in dread of a nuclear holocaust. I saw it again in a brilliant new production at the Northern Stage in Newcastle in 2010, when war raged in the Middle East.

Oh, What a Lovely War! honours the decent, ordinary folk who go to war, the medical staff who care for them, but it makes us laugh and quake at easy patriotism, false heroics, the vanity and slippery half-truths of politicians. It invites us to scoff at notions such as 'God is on our side', at tabloid 'gotcha' mentality, at media sentimentalization of soldiers' deaths. War is blood and slaughter, tragedy and grief, always has been and always will be. It can grow quickly from a collective stupidity that we must strive to resist.

Strongest memories of this work? The handsome young men turned into shuddering shell-shocked veterans on the stage, the multitude of white crosses stretching towards the horizon at the end of the film, and all those chippy cheerful yearning songs that spring from the core of life but are sung against a background of pain and death.

You'll see some of the songs from *Oh, What a Lovely War!* introducing the sections of this book.

LISSA EVANS – Author, producer and director

I once wrote a novel set during the Second World War; it was about the making of a film, and much of it took place in London, during the Blitz. What struck me most, during my research, was how much ordinary things went on mattering, even during extraordinary and terrible times. Being bombed nightly didn't stop people from wanting something nice for tea or being frustrated if a shoelace broke; it was the ordinary things that kept people anchored to the lives they'd had before, and which they hoped someday to have again.

Stanley Spencer knew this. He was an artist, but during the First World War he worked as a medical orderly, both in England and in northern Greece, where an obscure bit of the war was being fought. He saw many horrible things, brutal death and unspeakable injury; he saw men with shell shock, unable to cope with what they had seen and heard.

After the war, he was commissioned to paint the inside of the newly built Sandham Chapel. It's an extraordinary place, the walls completely filled with giant canvases that show a different war to the one normally portrayed: a shell-shocked soldier scrubbing a hospital corridor; early morning in a crowded tent, the soldiers shrouded in mosquito nets; a kit inspection; tea urns being filled; a medical orderly opening the gates of a hospital to let in a bus full of the wounded. Small, undramatic moments, but painted with as much intensity and detail as if they were battle scenes.

And in *Map Reading*, the painting I have chosen for this collection, Stanley Spencer showed something different again: a pause, a moment when the war could almost be forgotten.

The officer is using his horse as a map table. One of the soldiers is feeding the horse from a nosebag. No one else in the painting is doing any work at all – instead, they're snatching a few minutes in the sunshine. They're lolling, or sleeping, or picking berries from the mass of bushes at the top of the picture. For a brief moment, they can enjoy being ordinary people doing ordinary things. And in the end, that's what peace is really about.

Turn to the plate section in the middle of this book to see Lissa's choice in colour.

CLARE MORPURGO – Author and charity campaigner

Stanley Spencer was born in Cookham and lived there most of his life, painting many pictures of his beloved village.

In 1915, when he was twenty-two, Stanley volunteered to train with the Royal Army Medical Corps in Bristol, and in 1916 he served with the 68th Field Ambulance in Macedonia. In 1919 he painted *Travoys* to commemorate the First World War. He did not want his painting to glorify the horror of war but rather show a moment of redemption and peace.

Turn to the plate section in the middle of this book to see Clare's choice.

As a child I loved this picture long before I understood what it was about. The warm light shining from the stable seemed to be welcoming the travellers on their stretchers, with a promise of warmth and love. To me this could have been a Nativity scene, inspired by the legend that at midnight on Christmas Eve all the animals knelt down in their stables.

IAN BECK – Illustrator

When I first moved to London in the late 1960s I had a part-time job, two days a week at Harrods in Knightsbridge. I usually took the Tube to work but sometimes I would ride on the top deck of a bus. Going round Hyde Park Corner I was struck by the Royal Artillery Memorial. Fresh from art school I was surprised to find something so apparently 'old fashioned' and figurative so moving and involving. I was captivated by it and still am nearly fifty years later. I mentioned my interrest to a friend who said, 'I think the same sculptor did the wonderful soldier reading a letter at Paddington station.'

The next time I was at Paddington I made a point of seeking it out. It was obviously by the same hand. Instead of viewing the work from a distance, as in the case of the Artillery Memorial, it was possible to get close. The soldier is in battle dress. He has an army greatcoat draped over his shoulders. He is reading a letter from home. It appears to be winter as he has a home-knitted scarf tight around his neck. Perhaps the letter arrrived with the scarf, which was a Christmas present? His face is passive and his helmet is at a slightly rakish angle. This is a brief repite. A moment out of war. Time to catch up on the news from home. The image resonates as strongly today as it surely did when it was unveiled at 11 o'clock on Armistice Day in 1922.

Jagger himself fought in the trenches and was wounded twice. His soldiers are real and solidly imagined. His is an art born from experience. As Lord Churchill said at the unveiling, 'I can only hope that when you gaze upon it you may find some solace in the remembrance of those many letters that you wrote to your loved ones at the front, and that you will realise not only what a comfort they were to them, but also how they imbued them with fresh strength and fresh spirit to endure the many horrors and hardships of war.'

The Great Western Railway War Memorial
Sculpted by Charles Sargeant Jagger, 1922

EMMA THOMPSON – Actress, screenwriter and author

My father was mildly obsessed with the First World War. He owned a battered, brown-paper-covered facsimile of the *Wipers Times,* a newspaper written and produced in the trenches for and by the soldiers.

I used to pore over it for hours.

A great deal of it was funny. I particularly loved the cod adverts, Boarding Houses, strangely foretelling the tone of Spike Milligan and Monty Python.

The editors would beg their contributors for humorous pieces. The war made great poets of some, but there were clearly hundreds of others who longed to express their agony poetically but hadn't the gift.

'No more poetry!' would be the plaintive edict.

Produced under mind-bogglingly difficult circumstances, occasionally in some ghastly scramble from dugout to dugout, a printing block would go missing.

'All the "M"s in the issue to be represented by "W"s,' they'd warn – until some brave soul would risk all manner of hell to go back and find the missing letter.

Everything about this endeavour reveals the peculiarly bloody-minded stoicism of our tribe, determined to wring every morsel of humour out of sustained physical and moral catastrophe.

A DAY FROM THE LIFE OF A "SUB" IN DIVISIONAL RESERVE.

BY HIMSELF.

—o—o—o—

12·40 a.m.—Sleeping peacefully.

12·45 a.m.—Not sleeping peacefully.

12·50 a.m.—Awakened by a noise like a fog-horn gone quite mad.

12.55 a.m.—Realise someone has smelt gas, cannot find gas-helmet or shirt.

1 a.m.—Grope about for matches and candle—find out to my discomfort several extra articles of furniture in the hut—curse volubly.

1·5 a.m.—People rush in to remind me that I am orderly "bloke." Have heated altercation with "next for duty" as to when term of office ends. Matter settled by the entrance of C.O.—AM orderly officer.

1·15 a.m.—Stumble round camp—rumour of "Stand-to"—curse abominably.

1·30 a.m.—Rumour squashed—gas alarm false — somebody's clockwork motor-bike horn came unstuck—curse again—retire to bed.

3·30 a.m.—Sleeping peacefully.

3·35 a.m.—Alarming noise. Somebody with bigger feet than sense of decency, enters the hut; and knocks over a bully-beef box doing excellent work as a chair, collides with everybody's field-boots, mistakes my bed for his, and sits down on same . . . .

3·59 a.m.—Order restored by Company Commander.

6·0 a.m.—Reveillé.

6·30 a.m.—Get up, and wearily put on one or two garments, including somebody else's tie. Spend pleasant moments searching for my wandering collar stud.

7 a.m.—Go out and wave my limbs about for 45 minutes to the tune of "Head backward be-e-end."

7·45 a.m.—Try to shave—we have one mirror amongst six.

8 a.m.—Breakfast. The cook has plentifully peppered the sausage, put salt in my tea by mistake.

9 a.m.—Take party to and from the baths—one man has no cap badge—collect a bird from Adjutant. Have a bath myself, when nicely soaped the water gives out, becoming mud—curse offensively.

10 a.m.—Orderly room—attend with Company conduct sheets, collect another bird. Make arrangements for a cage and a supply of seed for same.

11 a.m.—Retire to hut and quaff a stoop of ale.

11·5 a.m.—Two in-command arrives inopportunely, speaks his mind and retires.

11·10 a.m.—Inspect my huts and men, their clothes, rifles, gas-helmets, feet, etc.

12 noon.—Realise I am not being as offensive as I might be, so go and annoy the next Company (who were working last night); by creeping in, starting their gramaphone with the loudest, longest and most loathed record, and creeping out again.

12·10 p.m.—Angry "sub" in pyjamas enters, am busy writing letters. After a few choice remarks about people in general and myself in particular, he goes away.

1 p.m.—Lunch.

2 p.m.—Sleeping peacefully.

4·30 p.m.—Tea.

5 p.m.—Fall in working party, astonishing number in my platoon suffer from bad feet at this hour. Discuss their ailment with them, and inspect members affected.

6·30 p.m.—Reach lorries and pack men in. No. 9999 Pte Jones X falls off and sprains his ankle, and proceeds to camp.

7·30 p.m.—Arrive at rendez-vous and await R.E.

8 p.m.—Await R.E.

9 p.m.—Await R.E.

9·15 p.m.—R.E. arrive in the shape of one most intelligent sapper.

9·30 p.m.—Loaded with material, proceed to job.

9·45 p.m.—My sergeant rushes up. Pte McNoodle, a sheet of corrugated iron, a duckboard, and a crump-hole full of water have got rather mixed. Leave a lance-corporal to straighten matters.

10 p.m.—German machine-gun annoying. Grateful for tin-hat.

1 a.m.—Return to lorries.

2 a.m.—Reach camp and retire to bed.

KLAUS FLUGGE – Publisher

It is perhaps not well known that a lot of German writers, and particularly poets, wrote about the First World War, many of them after the war, if they were lucky enough to survive.

Kurt Tucholsky, a great pacifist writer and journalist born in Berlin in 1880, was lucky, but committed suicide in 1935 in Sweden, having escaped from the Nazis in 1930. The sentiments expressed in this poem were often reflected in the letters my father wrote home from the front. He died at the end of the Second World War.

My own first experience of war took place during the nightly bombing of Hamburg in 1943 and, after my mother escaped from the burning city with her three children, in 1945 in East Germany.

I have always been an ardent pacifist despite brainwashing in school by both the Nazis and the Communists thereafter. The literature of the twenties in Germany produced a lot of great books and poems, anti-war and often pacifist, which had an influence on me for the rest of my life.

Prayer After the Slaughter

Heads off for prayer!

Oh God, our dirty and muddied old bones
Have crept forth once more from the trench's chalky stones.
We appear before you to pray and do not remain silent.

And ask you, Oh God:
Why?

Why have we given our heart's blood away?
While the Kaiser's six sons all living do stay.
We once believed . . . Oh how stupid we were . . . !
They made us all drunk . . .
Why?

One man screamed in his hospital bed for six months,
Before dry food and staff doctors finished him off.
Another became blind and took opium secretly.
Three of us between us have only one arm . . .
Why?

Faith, life, war and everything else we have lost
It was they, the powers, who tossed us into it
Like film gladiators.
We had the best audience,
But it didn't die with us.
Why? Why?

Lord God!
If you really are there as we daily do learn
Descend from starred heaven and show your concern!
Come down to us mortals or send us your son!
Tear the flags down, the orders, the decoration!
Announce to the countries of the earth how we have suffered;
How hunger, lice, shrapnel and lies our bodies have covered!
Chaplains have carried us to our graves in your name.
Declare they have lied! Is it us that you blame?

Chase us back to our graves, but answer us clear!
We kneel before you as best we can – but please lend us your
ear!
If our dying has not been completely without point,
Do not anoint us with another year like 1914!
Tell the people and drive them to desert!
A battalion of corpses looks to you for comfort.
All that remains for us is to come before you and pray!
Away!

Kurt Tucholsky

(*translated by* Peter Appelbaum)

JAMILA GAVIN – Writer

In the First World War 1.27 million Indians volunteered to fight for Britain. That is more than all the Scots, Welsh and Irish combined, and more than the sum total from all the rest of Britain's colonies and dominions.

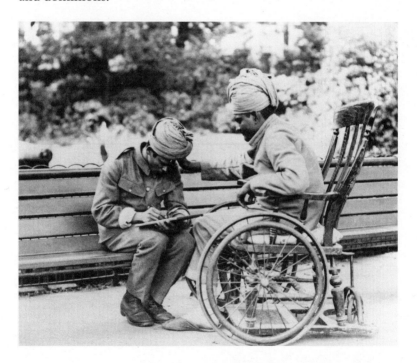

A wounded Punjabi soldier dictating a letter at a hospital in Brighton, August 1915

Do not think this is a war. This is not a war. It is the ending of the world. This is such a war as was related in the Mahabharata about our forefathers.

From a letter by a wounded Punjabi Rajput to a relative in India

A wounded Garhwali writes to his elder brother in India:

Twelve kings are fighting, but as yet, no victory has been achieved.

The twelve kings, among others, were:

Emperor George V of Great Britain and all his colonies
Kaiser Wilhelm II of Germany
Kaiser Franz Josef of the Austro-Hungarian Empire
Tsar Nicholas of Russia
King Peter of Serbia
King Ferdinand I of Bulgaria
King Constantine of Greece
King Vittorio Emanuele III of Italy
Prince Wilhelm zu Wied of Albania
King Haakon VII of Norway
King Christian X of Denmark
Sultan Mehmet V of Turkey

The experience of Indians fighting in the First World War was traumatic and revelatory. While their involvement was absolutely necessary to the British, who were otherwise greatly outnumbered by Germany and her allies, it presented Britain with a moral dilemma within the concept of white racial superiority, in which they believed completely: how could brown-skinned Indians be asked to kill the white-skinned enemy?

This nicety was overcome at first by deciding that only soldiers from the princely states should fight – and that the regiments should, by and large, be drawn from the northern states because it was believed that people from the South of India did not have the same fighting capacity and enthusiasm. The British thought this was because, for some Darwinian reason, the inhabitants of the South were racially inferior; probably because they tended to be darker and of shorter stature. Yet other reasons suggest it might be because the South had not experienced the constant invasions into the North going back three or more thousand years – by Greeks, Aryans, Mongols, Bactrians, Afghans, Turks, Scythians, Mughals and the British – which gave them a culture of warfare, as well as the consequent racial mixing. While the predominantly Hindu South had been spared the effect of many of these invasions, they had inherited much of the philosophy of the great Emperor Ashoka (273–232 BC) who, after a bloodthirsty start, embraced Buddhism and spent the rest of his reign promoting the concept of Dharma: respect for all life.

So the regiments which were sent to fight were largely drawn from the North – the Punjabis, Sikhs, Rajputs and Beluchis, the majority from Rawalpindi, now in Pakistan.

Khudadad Khan was the first Indian to receive the Victoria Cross for bravery. He fought with the 129th Duke of Connaught's Own Baluchis at the first Battle of Ypres, 1914.

They only plead for one reward,
Repaying every loss,
The right to wear like Britain's sons,
The great Victorian Cross.

Anon.

But even the many Indian regiments weren't enough for this war, which was devouring lives in their thousands, and there was forcible recruitment of young men from the towns and villages from across northern India – though persuasion was used as well.

The recruits are at your door step

Here you eat dried roti

There you'll eat fruit . . .

Here you are in tatters

There you'll wear a suit . . .

Here you wear worn out shoes

There you'll wear boot(s) . . .

Bhai Chhaila Patialewala

However, the conditions the soldiers found themselves in, especially those from the Indian regiments, were beyond their comprehension. They suffered dreadfully in uniforms best suited to the heat of India, and the carnage they witnessed could only be understood within their knowledge of the great epic battles of mythology in *The Mahabharata*; though the Chief Military Censor of letters commented: 'Not since the days of Hannibal has any body of mercenaries suffered so much and complained so little.' But the letters home were graphic.

> What you say in your letter about not being disloyal to the Emperor and it being the religion of Sikhs to die facing the foe – all that you say is true. But if only you yourself could be here and see for yourself! Any shrivelled Chars – Sodden fellow can fire the gun and kill a score of us at our food in the kitchen. Ships sail the sky like kites. Wherever you look, machine guns and cannon begin to shoot and bombs fly out which kill every man they hit.

The earth is mined and filled with powder; when men walk upon it, the powders is lit and up go the men! There is no fighting face to face. Guns massacre regiments sitting ten miles off. Put swords or pikes or staves in our hands and the enemy over us with like arms then indeed we should show you how to fight face to face! But if no one faces us what can we do? No one stands up to fight us. Everyone sits in a burrow underground. They fight in the sky, on the sea in battleships, under the earth in mines. My friend, a man who fights upon the ground can hardly escape. You tell me to fight face to the foe. Die we must — but alas, not facing the foe! My friend, the cannons are such that they throw a shell weighing twelve maunds (12×40 kgs) which destroys the earth five hundred paces round about where it falls. We are in France. It is a very cold country . . . It is a fair country and the people are like angels. All they lack is wings . . . The fighting is along a line of 300 miles. England, France, Italy, Belgium, Russia — these five are on one side; Germany, Turkey, Austria, Hungary, Bulgaria — these five on the other. The battle sways evenly balanced. None can kill the other. When it ends there will be peace. No one knows when this will be.

A Sikh writing in Gurmukhi from FPO 13, France, to Mahant Partab Das (Patiala State, Punjab) on 18 October 1915

> My dear brother, great damage has been caused to India.
> Nearly two hundred thousand men have been killed.
> About four thousand have lost arms and legs, and many
> have lost their sight ... all the world over there will
> be two women for each man ... All the kings have been
> ruined. Here an extraordinary amount of rain falls and
> the men's feet become frost bitten from the snow. Six
> months have passed since i saw the sun ...

A wounded Garhwali writing from hospital in England, 1917

Don't go don't go
Stay back my friend.

Crazy people are packing up,
Flowers are withering and friendships are breaking.
Stay back my friend.

Allah gives bread and work
You wouldn't find soothing shades anywhere else.
Don't go my friend, don't go.

Punjabi folk song of the early 20th century

The First World War was to shake up kingdoms, states, religions, customs and expectations of the whole world, from the great capitals and monarchies of Europe to the smallest of villages of India.

6th Cavalry, France, 28 August 1917

My prayer to you is that you will give up your foolish customs and extravagant expenses, and if you love your country will get others to follow your example. All our eyes have been opened since we came to this country. There are no beggars and no poor here. The country produces less than ours. Why then are they so much richer? Because they do not waste so much money on marriages, funerals and birth ceremonies, and do not put jewellery on their children. The children in India go about in ragged, torn clothes, and eat bread made of gram (chick peas,) and yet when they are married we spend thousands of rupees on the ceremony. Then comes the moneylender with his decree, and attaches the property, and we go out and wander about in search of employment to keep us alive. What we have to do is to educate our children, and if we do not we are fools, and our children will be fools also. Give up bad customs and value your girls as much as your boys.

Letter in Urdu from Ressaidar Bishan Singh (JAT 39) to Choudhuri Dobi Dyal (Jullundur District, Punjab)

Having breached one taboo – that of brown-skinned soldiers fighting white-skinned Germans – George V was keen to demonstrate his appreciation of the sacrifice so many Indians had made, and ordered that they should receive the finest nursing care in England. The Royal Pavilion, Brighton, was converted into hospital wards, in the hope that its oriental architecture would make them feel more at home. Of course, in view of the growing movement towards Indian independence now taking hold on the subcontinent, the British were also keen for soldiers returning to India to feel loyal to Britain.

The war at last was over . . .

From 'The King's Pilgrimage'

And there was neither paved highway,
   Nor secret path in the wood,
But had borne its weight of the broken clay
   And darkened 'neath the blood.

Father and mother they put aside,
   and the nearer love also –
An hundred thousand men who died
   whose graves shall no man know.

Rudyard Kipling

BALI RAI – Author

Often, as writers, we come across inspiration by accident. That's what happened before I wrote my novel *City of Ghosts* (2009), which is partly set during the Great War. I was reading a book called *Bloody Foreigners* by Robert Winder and came across a passage that surprised me. The author stated that one third of all the troops that fought for Britain during the First World War were from India. I was so shocked that I immediately started to research the topic. Not only was Mr Winder correct; apparently it was common knowledge. Not for me, it wasn't.

Back at school, we studied the Great War in history lessons, and the fantastic work of Wilfred Owen and Siegfried Sassoon in English. I was particularly taken by Sassoon's poem 'Dreamers' – a piece that opened my eyes to the everyday human tragedy of war. However, the one thing I wasn't taught about was the involvement of so many Indian troops – particularly Sikhs, which is my family's religion. I read letters from troops, learned all about the horrors of trench warfare, yet not once was I shown pictures of men who resembled my grandfather, walking into battle along French roads.

So, on commencing my research, I discovered two photographs that, in particular, inspired me to write my novel. The first was of Sikh troops marching in formation along a road in north-eastern France, close to Lille.

" Le 14 Juillet à **PARIS** en 1916 " — Les Cipayes Indiens

This image shows a local woman reaching across a Sikh soldier, possibly pinning something to his uniform. The man in question reminded me of my maternal grandfather, and so many other Sikh men. How strange a meeting it must have been – both for the Indian soldier and the local woman. How odd for her to see so many turban-wearing, bearded Sikhs marching through her town.

The image directly inspired passages in my novel, and a romance between my injured Sikh protagonist and his English nurse. It made me consider the everyday interaction between foreign troops and local people, much as Sassoon's poem framed soldiers on a more personal, human level in my mind.

The second image I found was equally important. It shows the town of Neuve Chapelle after a battle during March 1915. Most of the centre is desolate, charred and broken. Amidst the ruins, however, stands a crucifix – the church that once housed it completely destroyed.

NEUVE-CHAPELLE — Le Champ de Bataille — Le Christ des tranchées
The Christ of the trenches

This photograph inspired one of my favourite passages in *City of Ghosts*. The crucifix astounds my protagonist, Bissen Singh, weary after battle and charged with clearing out any remaining enemy troops. He wonders at its significance – and is reminded of his half-crazed grandmother and her tales:

> There were signs of God in everything, she said: in the warmth of a stranger's smile, and the flight of birds and the taste of a mango. In the waves of butterflies that erupted during the spring, and in the fat, life-giving droplets of rain that soaked you to the skin and made the gulleys and paths run with water.

Indian culture and Indian religions are, at their heart, fatalistic. The everyday things in life, and those bigger events such as birth, death and war, are meant to be – they are fate. For religious Indians, all incidents in life are the will of God. In that sense, the crucifix image linked directly to my protagonist's way of thinking and his belief system. In the midst of senseless slaughter and unprecedented destruction, Bissen saw a sign of hope. A sign that his God was watching over him and those he fought alongside. The image helped to shape my character. Without it, I'm not sure I would have written about Bissen at all.

Both these photographs, and others, encouraged me to reconnect with the First World War. I left school a long time ago, and it wasn't something I was particularly interested in writing about. That changed when I encountered these photographs. They lit a passion inside me, and pushed me to write about this shared British and Indian heritage – a period overlooked by far too many people. The historical link between India and Britain may be complex and multilayered, but it is also strong. The involvement of so many Indian troops during the war proved it. My British Asian (rather than Indian) heritage and culture, today, proves it. To have the chance to write about and explore that link, and to introduce a bit of hidden history to young-adult readers, was very welcome. That photographs taken in 1915 motivated me was serendipitous. Funny old thing, this inspiration malarkey . . .

SIR ROGER BANNISTER – Athlete and neurologist

My wife's mother joined the Queen Alexandra's Army Auxiliary Corps, and her first task was to take a troop of women around the country to commandeer hay from the farmers for the horses in France. Some tried to trick her by selling her straw.

She had a horse called Petrushka, and it could allegedly distinguish the difference in sound between an enemy aircraft and ours, and so the horse would come off the road towards the trees if the planes were German.

> ## FEAR GOD;
> ### honor your King and country;
> ### ABSTAIN FROM LIQUOR AND LOOTING;
> be courteous to women —
> but not more than courteous.

Kitchener's personal message to each British soldier

This clipping was found amongst her papers, cut from a Toronto newspaper in 1914. She had been working there, but then returned to England and became Captain – a deputy administrator in Queen Alexandra's Army Auxiliary Corps.

My mother-in-law was later awarded the MBE; her brother became Vice Chief of the Imperial General Staff, second only to Alan Brooke, having survived the First World War. Her other brother was killed on the Somme in August 1916.

MICHELLE MAGORIAN – Author

Sadly, many young boys had for years been encouraged to believe that the pinnacle of glory was to kill 'the enemy' for their country. Rudyard Kipling powerfully sums up this brainwashing in an epitaph:

COMMON FORM

> If any question why we died,
> Tell them, because our fathers lied.

Rudyard Kipling

Their deaths were far from glorious. Many of them, some only teenagers, died alone in the darkness of a muddy field, while in England children were encouraged to buy a tonic called Phosferine to send to the soldiers:

> You can imagine that I, as a gunner in the Tanks, have had an exciting time, as you would realise if you had seen the Megatherium creep across No Man's Land to give the Boche the fright of his life. I want to tell you that I have found Phosferine a really excellent nerve tonic for bracing up the whole nervous system and it needs it after being so

tremendously 'keyed up' during Tank operations, for there's no telling what will happen until it is all over and the reaction sets in. Phosferine is really excellent for dispensing the 'all out' feeling, and giving the strength and power necessary to resist all those insidious diseases that attack one who is exposed to all kinds of weather, and all those nerve-wracking experiences connected with the present campaign. I am as fit as a fiddle, and am convinced that my splendid condition is due in no small measure to Phosferine.

Gunner R. Mackintosh of the Heavy Branch Machine –
Gun Corps, British Expeditionary Force, who was in
the first advance of the tanks into the German lines

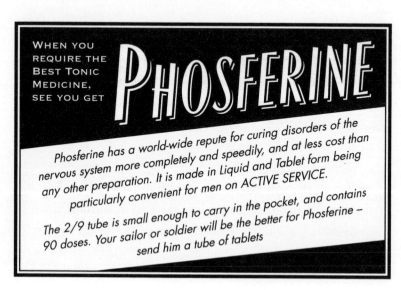

WHEN YOU REQUIRE THE BEST TONIC MEDICINE, SEE YOU GET **PHOSFERINE**

Phosferine has a world-wide repute for curing disorders of the nervous system more completely and speedily, and at less cost than any other preparation. It is made in Liquid and Tablet form being particularly convenient for men on ACTIVE SERVICE.

The 2/9 tube is small enough to carry in the pocket, and contains 90 doses. Your sailor or soldier will be the better for Phosferine – send him a tube of tablets

Taken from the December 1915 copy of My Magazine, a children's
paper edited by Arthur Mee

Meanwhile, thousands of these same soldiers were being used as decoys so that the enemy's attention was occupied while other troops manoeuvred themselves to a different area unchallenged. Carl Sandburg, in his poem 'Buttons', couldn't have put it more bluntly:

BUTTONS

I have been watching the war map slammed up for
advertising in front of the newspaper office.
Buttons – red and yellow buttons – blue and black buttons –
are shoved back and forth across the map.

A laughing young man, sunny with freckles,
Climbs a ladder, yells a joke to somebody in the crowd,
And then fixes a yellow button one inch west
And follows the yellow button with a black button one
inch west.

(Ten thousand men and boys twist on their bodies in
a red soak along a river edge,
Gasping of wounds, calling for water, some rattling
death in their throats.)
Who would guess what it cost to move two buttons one
inch on the war map here in front of the newspaper
office where the freckle-faced young man is laughing
to us?

Carl Sandburg

Risking their lives to care for these mutilated and shell-shocked men were the nurses. Under fire, they brought the wounded to the hospital ships off the coast of Gallipoli, worked on the front line and in casualty stations in France, or endured excessive temperatures in filthy disease-ridden tents in Salonika and the Middle East. They carried out new medical treatments on the survivors and comforted the dying, and they did it with calmness and dignity.

One of the most famous of these nurses was Edith Cavell. Her last words before she was executed were: 'I realize that patriotism is not enough, I must have no hatred or bitterness towards anyone.'

MARIELLA FROSTRUP – Journalist

These days we are far more familiar with images on screens than words on a page, and in this devastating poem Carol Ann Duffy uses a familiar device, the rewind button, to miraculously breathe life back into the millions of young lives lost in that terrible war. By refocusing us

Turn to page 124 for another poem by Carol Ann Duffy.

on what could have been, zooming in, not on the all too familiar images of slaughter but on the bittersweet possibilities of those lives unlived, she creates a heartbreaking vision of what should have been their destiny.

I'm particularly compelled by women's perspective on war; seldom instigators, or until recently active combatants, they have the capacity to shed a bright, unforgiving light on the hidden corners of the human tragedy. The fate of those brave young men on the battlefields is one cost of war, but also the millions of mothers and fathers, brothers and sisters, wives and girlfriends left wringing their hands, mourning boys they loved and trying to keep alive the memory of the sacrifices made in our name.

LAST POST

In all my dreams, before my helpless sight,
He plunges at me, guttering, choking, drowning.

This is a line from Wilfred Owen's 'Dulce et Decorum Est'. Turn to page 15 to read the whole poem.

If poetry could tell it backwards, true, begin
that moment shrapnel scythed you to the stinking mud . . .
but you get up, amazed, watch bled bad blood
run upwards from the slime into its wounds;
see lines and lines of British boys rewind
back to their trenches, kiss the photographs from home—
mothers, sweethearts, sisters, younger brothers
not entering the story now
to die and die and die.
Dulce – No – Decorum – No – Pro patria mori.
You walk away.

You walk away; drop your gun (fixed bayonet)
like all your mates do too—
Harry, Tommy, Wilfred, Edward, Bert—
and light a cigarette.
There's coffee in the square,
warm French bread
and all those thousands dead
are shaking dried mud from their hair
and queuing up for home. Freshly alive,
a lad plays Tipperary to the crowd, released
from History; the glistening, healthy horses fit for heroes, kings.

You lean against a wall,
your several million lives still possible
and crammed with love, work, children, talent, English beer,
good food.
You see the poet tuck away his pocket-book and smile.
If poetry could truly tell it backwards, then it would.

Carol Ann Duffy

JOHN BOYNE – Novelist

I've written two novels set during the First World War: *The Absolutist* (2011) and *Stay Where You Are and Then Leave* (2013), the former written for adult readers, the latter for younger.

It's a period that continues to fascinate me, perhaps because I still understand it less than I do the Second World War, which has a recognizable evil in the form of Adolf Hitler and an unparalleled atrocity in the Holocaust. The First World War, however, is not as easy to define or understand; I think most people would struggle even to name the main antagonists.

When we think of the First World War, we think of location more than politics. We think of the trenches and the barbed wire. We think of poppies and dead young bodies scattered across no man's land. And, if we are truly concerned with acts of bravery, we think of conscientious objectors.

Between researching and writing these two novels, I came across a poem by the former Poet Laureate, Andrew Motion, titled 'The Death of Harry Patch'.

Turn to page 205 for Sir Andrew Motion's own selection.

Patch, the last fighting Tommy, was conscripted in 1916, fought at the Battle of Passchendaele and died, the final surviving British soldier from the First World War, at the age of 111 in 2009.

Motion's poem achieves its great power through the image of hundreds of thousands of dead soldiers rising from the 'ruined ground', falling into line with each other while leaving a single space to complete their number: Harry Patch – 'but this is him now, running quick-sharp along the duckboards'. There's a sense that when all the soldiers are finally reunited, unity is achieved. And completeness. And even, perhaps, peace.

THE DEATH OF HARRY PATCH

When the next morning eventually breaks,
a young Captain climbs onto the fire step,
knocks ash from his pipe then drops it
still warm into his pocket, checks his watch,
and places the whistle back between his lips.

At 6.00 hours precisely, he gives the signal,
but today nothing that happens next happens
according to plan. A very long and gentle note
wanders away from him over the ruined ground
and hundreds of thousands of dead who lie there

immediately rise up, straightening their tunics
before falling in as they used to do, shoulder
to shoulder, eyes front. They have left a space
for the last recruit of all to join them: Harry Patch,
one hundred and eleven years old, but this is him

now, running quick-sharp along the duckboards.
When he has taken his place, and the whole company
are settled at last, their padre appears out of nowhere,
pausing a moment in front of each and every one
to slip a wafer of dry mud onto their tongues.

Andrew Motion

HOWARD GOODALL – Composer

I chose this beautiful, haunting poem by Canadian military doctor and poet John McCrae as the text of the sixth movement, *Dies Irae*, in my *Eternal Light: A Requiem* (2008); I did so, not just because it is full of a deep and personal compassion for the fallen (it was written just after McCrae had buried a friend), but because, unusually, it is written as if the dead themselves are speaking from beyond their graves.

It seemed to me that singing would be a perfect way to give them voice a century or so later. This poem is one of the origins of the tradition of commemorating the huge human losses of that and subsequent wars with poppies, as McCrae was one of many at the time who noticed that poppies grew so quickly from the graves of soldiers in First World War Flanders. When *Eternal Light: A Requiem* was first performed in its dance version by Rambert, the dance company, it was portrayed with astonishing delicacy in a deep, red glow of light, the bodies of the dancers representing not just the souls of the departed but the gently swaying poppies above their resting place.

In Flanders Fields

In Flanders fields the poppies blow
Between the crosses, row on row,
That mark our place; and in the sky
The larks, still bravely singing, fly
Scarce heard amid the guns below.

We are the Dead. Short days ago
We lived, felt dawn, saw sunset glow,
Loved and were loved, and now we lie
In Flanders fields.

Take up our quarrel with the foe:
To you from failing hands we throw
The torch; be yours to hold it high.
If ye break faith with us who die
We shall not sleep, though poppies grow
In Flanders fields.

John McCrae

HER ROYAL HIGHNESS THE DUCHESS OF CORNWALL

My three great-uncles were all killed at the Somme within six weeks of each other. I cannot imagine what it must have been like for my great-grandparents to receive such devastating news. It is so hard for us, a century later, to understand what the soldiers of the Great War and their families went through.

For this anthology I have chosen 'The Christmas Truce' by the Poet Laureate, Carol Ann Duffy. It is about the spontaneous, unofficial ceasefire between British and German troops along the Western Front on Christmas Day. Huddled in flooded, freezing trenches; facing each other over the hideous shell-holes and barbed wire of no-man's-land, it was a moment when both sides recognized what united them as men, rather than what divided them as soldiers.

Poetry is like time travel, and poems take us to the heart of the matter. This poem made me cry. It is such a touching and perceptive evocation – through its deceptively simple language and powerful imagery – of the truth of life in the trenches, and of that moment of hope when the sounds of war were silenced.

THE CHRISTMAS TRUCE

Christmas Eve in the trenches of France,
the guns were quiet.
The dead lay still in No Man's Land –
Freddie, Franz, Friedrich, Frank . . .
The moon, like a medal, hung in the clear, cold sky.

Silver frost on barbed wire, strange tinsel,
sparkled and winked.
A boy from Stroud stared at a star
to meet his mother's eyesight there.
An owl swooped on a rat on the glove of a corpse.

In a copse of trees behind the lines,
a lone bird sang.
A soldier-poet noted it down – *a robin*
holding his winter ground –
then silence spread and touched each man like a hand.

Somebody kissed the gold of his ring;
a few lit pipes;
most, in their greatcoats, huddled,
waiting for sleep.
The liquid mud had hardened at last in the freeze.

But it was Christmas Eve; *believe*; belief
thrilled the night air,
where glittering rime on unburied sons
treasured their stiff hair.

The sharp, clean, midwinter smell held memory.
On watch, a rifleman scoured the terrain –
no sign of life,
no shadows, shots from snipers,
nowt to note or report.
The frozen, foreign fields were acres of pain.

Then flickering flames from the other side
danced in his eyes,
as Christmas Trees in their dozens shone,
candlelit on the parapets,
and they started to sing, all down the German lines.

Men who would drown in mud, be gassed, or shot,
or vaporised
by falling shells, or live to tell,
heard for the first time then –
*Stille Nacht. Heilige Nacht. Alles schläft, einsam
wacht . . .*

*Cariad, the song was a sudden bridge
from man to man;
a gift to the heart from home,
or childhood, some place shared . . .*
When it was done, the British soldiers cheered.

A Scotsman started to bawl *The First Noel*
and all joined in,
till the Germans stood, seeing
across the divide,
the sprawled, mute shapes of those who had died.

All night, along the Western Front, they sang,
the enemies –
carols, hymns, folk songs, anthems,
in German, English, French;
each battalion choired in its grim trench.

So Christmas dawned, wrapped in mist,
to open itself
and offer the day like a gift
for Harry, Hugo, Hermann, Henry, Heinz . . .
with whistles, waves, cheers, shouts, laughs.

Frohe Weihnachten, Tommy! Merry Christmas, Fritz!
A young Berliner,
brandishing schnapps,
was the first from his ditch to climb.
A Shropshire lad ran at him like a rhyme.

Then it was up and over, every man,
to shake the hand
of a foe as a friend,
or slap his back like a brother would;
exchanging gifts of biscuits, tea, Maconochie's stew,

Tickler's jam . . . for cognac, sausages, cigars,
beer, sauerkraut;
or chase six hares, who jumped
from a cabbage-patch, or find a ball
and make of a battleground a football pitch.

I showed him a picture of my wife.
Ich zeigte ihm
ein Foto meiner Frau.
Sie sei schön, sagte er.
He thought her beautiful, he said.

They buried the dead then, hacked spades
into hard earth
again and again, till a score of men
were at rest, identified, blessed.
Der Herr ist mein Hirt . . . *my shepherd, I shall not want.*

And all that marvellous, festive day and night,
they came and went,
the officers, the rank and file,
their fallen comrades side by side
beneath the makeshift crosses of midwinter graves . . .

. . . beneath the shivering, shy stars
and the pinned moon
and the yawn of History;
the high, bright bullets
which each man later only aimed at the sky.

Carol Ann Duffy

MICHAEL FOREMAN – Illustrator

Two brothers walked out of my grandfather's little Suffolk cottage in 1914 and went to war. Their names are on the village war memorial. A third brother, my father, was too young to go with them.

At the same time, two other young men, my mother's brothers, left Granny's Norfolk pub and went to war. Their names are on another war memorial.

There are no photographs of these young men. They didn't live long enough to have children. They left just four names amid a multitude. But they have always been part of our family, woven into the patchwork of memory and story.

When writing my childhood memories in *War Boy*, I was conscious of this lost generation, and wrote *War Game* as a tribute to them.

Turn to the plate section in the middle of this book to see Michael's choice in colour.

The order was given to counter-attack, to try to take the German trenches before they could reorganize themselves. Will and the rest of the British soldiers scrambled over the parapet.

Freddie still had the football! He drop-kicked it far into the mist of No Man's Land.

'That'll give someone a surprise,' he said.

'Why are goalies always daft?' thought Will.

They were on the attack. Running in a line, Will in a centre forward position, Lacey to his left, young Billy on the wing.

From the corner of his eye Will saw Freddie dive full-length, then curl up as if clutching a ball in the best goalkeeping tradition.

'Daft as a brush,' Will thought.

Suddenly they all seemed to be tackled at once. The whole line went down. Earth and sky turned over, and Will found himself in a shell hole staring at the sky. Then everything went black.

Slowly the blackness cleared and Will could see the hazy sky once more. Bits of him felt hot and other bits felt very cold. He couldn't move his legs. He heard a slight movement. There was someone else in the shell hole.

Will dimly recognized the gleam of a fixed bayonet and the outline of a German.

'Wasser. Wasser,' the German said.

It was about the only German word Will knew. He fumbled for his water bottle and managed to push it towards the German with the butt of his rifle. The German drank deeply. He didn't have the strength to return the bottle.

'Kinder?' he said. Will shook his head. The German held up three fingers. Will tried to shake his head again to show that he did not understand, but the blackness returned.

Later he saw a pale ball of gold in the misty sky.

'There's a ball in Heaven,' he thought. 'Thank God. We'll all have a game when this nightmare's over.'

At home when he had a bad dream he knew that if he opened his eyes, the bad dream would end. But here, his eyes were already open.

Perhaps if he closed them, the nightmare would end.

He closed his eyes.

Michael Foreman

AT HOME

Keep the Home Fires Burning

They were summoned from the hillside,
They were called in from the glen,
And the the country found them ready
At the stirring call for men.
Let no tears add to their hardships
As the soldiers march along,
And although your heart is breaking,
Make it sing this cheery song.

Keep the home fires burning,
While your hearts are yearning.
Though the lads are far away,
They dream of home.
There's a silver lining
Through the dark clouds shining,
Turn the dark cloud inside out.
Till the boys come home.

FROM *PRIVATE PEACEFUL*

As I came round the corner I saw them. Behind the band there must have been a couple of dozen soldiers, splendid in their scarlet uniforms. They marched past me, arms swinging in perfect time, buttons and boots shining, the sun glinting on their bayonets. They were singing along with the band: *It's a long way to Tipperary, it's a long way to go.* And I remember thinking it was a good thing Big Joe wasn't there, because he'd have been bound to join in with his *Oranges and Lemons.* Children were stomping alongside them, some in paper hats, some with wooden sticks over their shoulders. And there were women throwing flowers, roses mostly, that were falling at the soldiers' feet. But one of them landed on a soldier's tunic and somehow stuck there. I saw him smile at that.

Like everyone else, I followed them round the town and up into the square. The band played *God Save the King* and then, with the Union Jack fluttering behind him, the first sergeant major I'd ever set eyes on got up on to the steps of the cross, slipped his stick smartly under his arm, and spoke to us, his voice unlike any voice I'd heard before: rasping, commanding.

'I shan't beat about the bush, ladies and gentlemen,' he began. 'I shan't tell you it's all tickety-boo out there in France – there's been too much of that nonsense already in my view. I've been there. I've seen it for myself. So I'll tell you straight. It's no picnic. It's hard slog, that's what it is, hard slog. Only one question to ask yourself about this war. Who would you rather see marching through your streets? Us lot or the Hun? Make up your minds. Because, mark my words, ladies and gentlemen, if we don't stop them out in France the Germans will be here, right here in Hatherleigh, right here on your doorstep.'

I could feel the silence all around.

'They'll come marching through here burning your houses, killing your children, and yes, violating your women. They've beaten brave little Belgium, swallowed her up in one gulp. And now they've taken a fair slice of France too. I'm here to tell you that unless we beat them at their own game, they'll gobble us up as well.' His eyes raked over us. 'Well? Do you want the Hun here? Do you?'

'No!' came the shout, and I was shouting along with them.

'Shall we knock the stuffing out of them then?'

'Yes!' we roared in unison.

The sergeant major nodded. 'Good. Very good. Then we shall need you.' He was pointing his stick now into the crowd, picking out the men. 'You, and you and you.' He was looking straight at me now, into my eyes. 'And you too, my lad!'

Until that very moment it had honestly never occurred to me that what he was saying had anything to do with me. I had been an onlooker. No longer.

'Your king needs you. Your country needs you. And all the brave lads out in France need you too.' His face broke into a smile as he fingered his immaculate moustache. 'And remember one thing, lads – and I can vouch for this – all the girls love a soldier.'

The ladies in the crowd all laughed and giggled at that. Then the sergeant major returned the stick under his arm. 'So, who'll be the first brave lad to come up and take the king's shilling?'

No one moved. No one spoke up. 'Who'll lead the way? Come along now. Don't let me down, lads. I'm looking for boys with hearts of oak, lads who love their King and their country, brave boys who hate the lousy Hun.'

That was the moment the first one stepped forward, flourishing his hat as he pushed his way through the cheering crowd. I knew him at once from school. It was big Jimmy Parsons. I hadn't seen him for a while, not since his family had moved away from the village. He was even bigger than I remembered, fuller in the face and neck, and redder too. He was showing off now just like he always had done in the school yard. Egged on by the crowd, others soon followed.

Suddenly someone prodded me hard in the small of my back. It was a toothless old lady pointing at me with her crooked finger. 'Go on, son,' she croaked. 'You go and fight. It's every man's duty to fight when his country calls, that's what I say. Go on. Y'ain't a coward, are you?'

Everyone seemed to be looking at me then, urging me on, their eyes accusing me as I hesitated. The toothless old lady jabbed me again, and then she was pushing me forward. 'Y'ain't a coward, are you? Y'ain't a coward?' I didn't run, not at first. I sidled away from her slowly, and then backed out of the crowd hoping no one would notice me. But she did. 'Chicken!' she screamed after me. 'Chicken!' Then I did run. I ran helter-skelter down the deserted High Street, her words still ringing in my ears.

Michael Morpurgo

JAMES PATTERSON – Author

Of course, the horror of war wasn't felt only on the battlefield but at home too, in the impact it had on the lives of those left behind: the parents, the wives and the children.

In *Lord of the Nutcracker Men*, ten-year-old Johnny loves to play with the army of nutcracker soldiers his father makes for him. But when Johnny's father enlists to fight, the letters he writes home, although cheerful at first, soon begin to tell his son too much about the ugly truth of war, and Johnny must come to terms with the fact that war is no longer just a game. *Lord of the Nutcracker Men* is included on the required reading lists of many American schools, and rightly so.

FROM *LORD OF THE NUTCRACKER MEN*

November 2, 1914

Dearest Johnny,

I like to think that I've never lied to you before, but once I did. It was just a little lie, but you caught me at it – do you remember? At that moment, when I saw the look in your eyes, I promised myself that I would never lie to you again.

Well, right now it's very hard. I think of you there in the house where I grew up and see you as a child playing beneath that enormous tree. I want so badly to tell you that everything is fine, that I'm having a splendid adventure, and that you shouldn't worry about me. But then I remember that you're ten years old now, not really a child at all, though not quite yet a man. And it wouldn't be fair to you or me to tell you simple things like that.

The truth is, Johnny, that I'm crouched in the mud like an animal, and the man at my side is crying and holding himself, and there is nothing between us and the Boche but fifty yards of the most haunted ground I have ever imagined. I have seen it only in the flashes of star shells, but it looks even worse for that, I think. In the fizzly light of the flares it is utterly white or utterly black, with no shadows in between.

We came up to the line in a great rush, in the dead of night, running through the mud with our rifles and our packs. It is now the hour before the dawn. Old Fritz's guns are hammering at our trenches, and ours are battering his. The shells pass overhead with eerie ripping sounds, as though the sky is shredding into pieces. His guns twinkle far ahead, and ours flash behind us. But in the middle there is darkness, until a star shell bursts and flutters down. Then we see the ground heaving up, the dirt and mud all tossed about, and it looks like the Channel on a windy day, the earth a stormy sea.

The sound is tremendous. It shakes the air.

As you might suppose, I haven't had much sleep. I've spent the night carving a little officer, enclosed. It will be up to him to lead us over the top when we march against old Fritz.

The lads think I have nerves of steel to sit here carving and painting. But I find it rather relaxing.

I have to hurry now, as in just a few minutes we'll get the order to stand to. I don't know yet what the day will bring, but it can't be worse than the darkness.

I miss you very much.

All my love,

Dad

Iain Lawrence

DAME JACQUELINE WILSON – Author

My favourite author when I was a child was Noel Streatfeild. I read *Ballet Shoes* so often I practically knew it by heart (and for years I gambolled about our flat in my pink bedroom slippers, pretending they were proper ballet shoes).

I bought her autobiography, *A Vicarage Family*, and read it with enormous interest. Noel writes about her parents and brother and sisters – and her cousin, John. He's an intellectual, sensitive boy, who hates sport and wants to be an actor. As a schoolboy he says, 'Dad says I'm not manly – I'm not, anything disgusting makes me ill, when a boy was sick in chapel I fainted.'

It's therefore a particularly dreadful ordeal for John when he has to go and fight in France in 1914. Noel Streatfeild writes about what happens to him in just three pages at the end of her book. They're simple and understated, but it shows children the full horror of the First World War in an indelible way.

FROM *A VICARAGE FAMILY*

There was to be no acting for John. That summer on the 4th of August war was declared against Germany. And John, already a partly trained territorial, after a few months of more intensive training, was sent to France.

The ordinary English man and woman knew nothing about war. That it would all be over soon was the first reaction. It was not in any case expected to affect the lives of the ordinary citizen. Wars were fought by soldiers and sailors, who came on leave and were made a fuss of.

But it soon became apparent this war was not like that. People became nervous. 'I don't like the Vicar to be away even for a night,' a woman said. 'For what would we do if those Germans landed?'

That first winter fuel was either scarce or expensive – the girls did not know which, but before school Victoria and Louise had to saw logs.

'I haven't done this,' said Victoria, 'since I had to do it as a punishment for that awful report.'

Food grew scarce. They kept hens in the field where it had been planned Isobel should have a studio. Isobel put an ostrich egg they had been given as a curio in the hen house and painted a Union Jack over it, writing under it: 'A German hen laid this, now see what you can do.'

Then came the casualties. House after house opened as a hospital. Isobel, when she was well enough, worked in one as a ward maid. But somehow for the girls the war remained remote. Life went on more or less the same, except that there were no dances for Isobel, indeed, no parties for any of them.

Then John came on leave. The moment the news got round that he was coming presents of food arrived, among them a large rabbit.

'Would you lend me that for a day, Mrs Strangeway, ma'am?' the butcher said when he was asked to clean it. 'I'll hang it in my window. It encourages people just to see food about.'

Victoria was at school when John came home. It was June and lovely weather.

'He's in the garden,' her mother said to her when she came in. 'I think he looks peaky.'

John was in that part of the garden the children had
christened The Wood. He was in uniform with the star of a
second lieutenant on his shoulder. He looked more than peaky:
he looked thin, and his face was green. But he sounded in a
way the old John.

'Hullo, Vicky! How's things?'

Victoria felt as if a cold hand had squeezed her heart.

'You look pretty awful.'

John managed a smile.

'I've just been sick under the bushes there. It's nothing.'

'Why were you sick? Have you eaten something bad?'

'Don't talk about it to the family but I'm sick rather a lot.'

She stared up at him. Then, why she did not know, she put
a hand on his arm.

'Tell me.'

It was then the dreadful thing happened. John, the self-
contained, the poised, broke down. Tears rolled down his cheeks.

'Oh, Vicky. You'll never know how awful it is.'

Suddenly she felt old.

'Tell me. Tell me every single thing.'

So he told her. Of the squelching mud. The unburied bodies.
The dying, screaming on barbed wire. The filth. The lice. The
smells. Then, retching as he remembered, he whispered:

'And oh, Vicky, I have to go back.'

Somehow between them she and John managed to keep to
themselves that there was anything wrong with him other than
fatigue. Victoria sent a pink note to Miss French:

'Please,' she said, 'I must miss school while John's on leave.
We've always done things together. You do see, don't you.'

Miss French must have seen, for all she said was:

'Get your things on, dear. I will send a note to your parents.'

So with Spot, John and Victoria went for long walks over the downs; and though distant thuds sounded from the guns across the Channel, the air was fresh and clear, and after the exercise even John was able to enjoy a meal at a cottage table.

They never again spoke of conditions at the front. Instead, they lived entirely in the past. It was always: 'Do you remember?'

The day his leave finished John refused to be seen off at the station. He had to catch an early train to link up with the troop train at Victoria.

'I don't want to be seen off. Just all come to the door. I'd like that.'

So, as his taxi drove away, they were all there. The family, Annie, Hester and Spot. Perhaps he carried that picture to France.

Five weeks later the telegram came. Victoria knew something was wrong when she came in from sawing logs and saw Annie, her apron over her head, sobbing behind the kitchen door.

Her father called her into his study. 'I don't know how to tell you, Vicky darling. You are so young to face sorrow.'

Victoria gently stroked her father's hand.

'It's John. He's been killed.'

'Yes, Vicky.'

She stared unseeingly out of the window towards the front gate.

'I'll be all right, Daddy. I think I knew it was going to happen. Grand-Nanny once said growing up came suddenly. I grew up all in one minute, the day John came on leave.'

Noel Streatfeild

THERESA BRESLIN – Author

Much of what has been written about the First World War is for, and about, an older readership, so I am thrilled that this anthology is for younger readers.

Doing research for the books and stories I've written about the First World War (*Remembrance*, *Act of Love*, *Ghost Soldier*), I read letters and diaries, and visited museums, memorials and battlefields.

This article in *The Times* tells us that, under certain conditions, the army will now accept underage and illiterate soldiers.

THE TIMES, WEDNESDAY, OCTOBER 13, 1915

RECRUITING RULES RELAXED.

EDUCATION TEST DROPPED.

There are indications that under the new Director of Recruiting the enlistment rules will be relaxed in various directions.

The Procurator-Fiscal at Haddington has received a letter from the Director of Recruiting on the subject of a man who was refused enlistment because he could not read or write. The letter says :—

It is now proposed to relax the regulations on this subject, so far as it concerns enlistment for the duration of the war, in the case of infantry and certain other branches of the Army in which a standard of literacy is not essential, and steps are being taken to issue the necessary orders to all recruiting officials.

Until quite recently boys of 17 who enlisted without the consent of their parents were liable to be discharged on the application of their parents. The War Office have now announced that once a youth enters the Army, provided he is not under 17, he is to be kept in the service, and further, if the medical officer certifies that he is physically up to the standard of 18½ years, he may be sent to active service abroad.

In the House of Commons yesterday, Mr. Tennant said that no cases of under-age enlistment had come to the notice of the War Office since the instructions issued last June.

News in Brief.

Minimum rates of wages have been fixed for tin box and canister-making trade.

Only 14,000 school children are now receiving meals in London as compared with 74,000 a year.

In accordance with custom an ox was roasted in the street at Stratford-on-Avon on the occasion of the "Mop Fair," the ancient hiring fair of the district.

By the demolition of old property at Carlisle in the neighbourhood of the Castle, some 50ft. of the city wall has been uncovered.

Hampton District Council has decided to present the 3rd Battalion, Surrey Volunteer Training the Boer rifles presented to the parish by Lord Roberts after the South African War.

The Higher Education Sub-Committee of the London County Council recommends that no action in the matter of the site for the University of London should be taken during the period of the war.

The death is announced of the Rev. Stuart Townley, vicar of Emmanuel Church, South formerly headmaster of Sussex House School, Se and vicar of Teynham, Kent.

At a sale of rare postage stamps at the gallery of Messrs. Glendining and Co., Argyll-street, a fine unused copy of a 1d. vermilion stamp Cape of Good Hope (1861) was sold for £9 15s.

Mr. Charles Lupton, chairman and treasurer Leeds Infirmary Board, has accepted the office Lord Mayor of Leeds. Mrs. Lupton is a sister of Ashton of Hyde and Lady Bryce.

The Bishop of Durham's motor-car driver was fined £2 at the Durham City Police Court for driving a car to which the lights attached were of excessive brightness.

An officer's diary
reveals his compassion
for his men and his
awareness of the failure
of the attack of 1 July on
the Somme, where he
notes the colossal loss
of life.

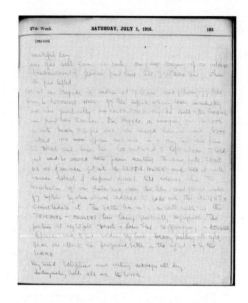

Compare this to the
report of the same battle
in the *War Illustrated*,
which tells us:

*But we are advancing!
I doubt if anyone who
has not lived with
fighting armies can
understand the thrill
of this phrase, the fresh
enthusiasm that sweeps
over the ranks, the
triumphant emotion it
brings. Losses seem to
count for nothing . . .*

This was the inspiration for the character of Alex, the young lad in *Remembrance,* who lies about his age in order to enlist to seek revenge for the death of his brother; and for Jack, the shepherd lad who went to war, in *Ghost Soldier.*

Ghost Soldier is a story of how the war affected young children on the home front – our youth who became the future. In the book Rob, a young boy searching for his missing father, climbs aboard a hospital train bringing the wounded into Edinburgh. Rob has heard adults talking positively about the progress of the war and has seen images of brave soldiers in magazines, such as *War Illustrated.* His father's letters home tell of the camaraderie of the men and glorious sights of an army on the move, singing as they march along. Sending his little sister, Millie, to get on the train at the rear, Rob moves through the train from the front. He is shocked at the state of the men and their dreadful wounds: victims of gas attacks and those with limbs amputated. In a special carriage at the end of the train he comes face to face with a shell-shocked and traumatized Jack, who is holding a loaded gun to Millie's head . . .

FROM *GHOST SOLDIER*

'Millie!' Rob gasped.

'Robbie,' Millie whispered. 'I knew you'd come to save me.'

Rob stared at her, and then at the young lad with the pistol. The boy's face was dirty grey with a mottled flush high on each cheek. His eyes were red-rimmed and they flashed about, never still.

Rob had cared for farm animals all his life. Normally they were very biddable, but if the sheep were sick or lambing, or a cow was with calf, they became unpredictable, and therefore dangerous – sometimes extremely dangerous. His dad had told him it was because they were frightened and in pain, and the best way to handle them was to try to understand what they were suffering. One bleak night on the hills they had birthed a lamb from a sick ewe. Hunkered down, his father stroked the writhing creature, teaching Rob how to gentle her into allowing him to help: 'Think how you would like to be treated if you were scared and didn't know what was happening to you.'

The lad in front of him was shaking, his whole body trembling so much he could hardly hold the gun steady. Rob felt fear rising in his throat as he realized that the gun might go off and his sister would be killed. And there was nothing he could do.

Apart from what his father might have done.

WIRE by Paul Nash.

MAP READING *by Stanley Spencer. Turn to page 86 to read Lissa Evans's introduction.*

GASSED by John Singer Sargent. Turn to page 201 to read Shirley Hughes's introduction.

TRAVOYS ARRIVING WITH WOUNDED AT A DRESSING-STATION AT SMOL, MACEDONIA, SEPTEMBER 1916 by Stanley Spencer. Turn to page 87 to read Clare Morpurgo's introduction.

From WAR GAME *by Michael Foreman.*
Turn to pages 129-131 to read an extract and Michael's introduction.

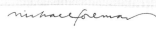

CANARY by Emma Chichester Clark.
Turn to page 29 to read Emma's introduction to BIRDSONG by Sebastian Faulks.

FRENCH TROOPS RESTING by Christopher Nevinson.

Rob stepped back, creating a space between himself and the lad. 'It's all right,' he said softly. He held his hands out, palms up. 'It's all right,' he repeated.

He relaxed his body and saw the lad relax slightly too.

'I'm not going to hurt you,' Rob said in the same soft voice. 'I'm not going to do anything at all.'

Behind him the carriage door crashed open. A voice roaring a command. Chesney's voice.

'You! Farm boy. Out of here. At once!'

Without turning round, Rob shook his head. 'I'm not leaving my sister.'

'I told you,' Chesney said through gritted teeth, 'not to get on the train. Now I'm telling you to move aside. Do it!'

'He stays.' The lad with the pistol addressed Chesney. 'But you! You get out of here or I'll blow your head off! I mean it!' He pointed the gun at the orderly. 'Get out or I'll fire this gun at you!'

There was a silence; then Chesney leaned forward and hissed in Rob's ear, 'If you don't leave I'll have your soldier father put on a charge and locked up for years.'

'You can't put Daddy on a charge and lock him up.' To Rob's astonishment, it was Millie who spoke up. 'He's missing in the war and that's why we're here. To find out if he's on this train.'

'You shouldn't *be* on this train,' Chesney snapped at her.

'Medical orderly! Stand down!'

An army officer and the nurse had appeared at the carriage door.

'Sir,' Chesney protested. 'This boy disobeyed instructions.'

'Stand down,' the officer repeated. 'That's an order.'

Chesney glared at Rob. When he'd gone, the officer leaned

against the door, looked around, and then said in mild tones, 'My name is Captain Morrison. I'd be obliged if someone would bring me up to date on this situation.'

There was a silence.

'Anyone at all? Please.'

The soldier tied to the metal rail stopped mumbling and spoke up without opening his eyes. 'Soldier Jack the Lad here is really good at nicking things. Handcuff keys, guns, and such like. He's been planning his escape ever since we got on at Folkestone. When the train stopped, he was ready to leg it when this little girl turns up asking questions about where the regiments are posted. So he decides she's a German spy and—'

'A German spy.' The lad with the gun tightened his grip on the pistol.

'I'm not a German spy!' Millie squeaked.

Nell's tail was down. Until now she'd had the good sense not to make a noise. But reacting to the alarm in Millie's voice, she crouched, growling low in her throat.

'Quiet, Nell,' said Rob.

The lad with the gun gave a start and looked down at the dog. 'Nell?' he said. The gun wavered in his hand. 'Nell?'

Then the most startling thing happened. Nell stood up and wagged her tail.

'Nell,' the boy said again, more confidently.

And to Rob's amazement, Nell trotted forward to stand quite happily beside the young soldier.

'I could look after that gun for you, son.'

Captain Morrison was first to recover. He held out his hand. The young lad unclenched his grip on the pistol and the officer took it carefully from him.

Rob looked at the floor. He didn't want to see what happened next. He knew enough about the army to realize that a soldier who threatened an officer with a gun would be arrested and shot at dawn.

But the captain slipped the gun inside his tunic and said to the nurse, 'Give our young soldier some of those knockout drops you reserve for emergencies. When he's being assessed in Edinburgh, I'll see if we can get him admitted to a psychiatric unit somewhere. Maybe some smart doctor can straighten out his brain. And – oh,' he added, 'I suggest you put a note in his record that he has a special skill for . . . how shall we put it? . . . appropriating unattended objects.' He touched his cap to the nurse and left.

The lad was kneeling beside Nell, stroking her coat as though it were the most natural thing in the world.

The nurse and Bert came into the carriage. The nurse said, 'Bert will look after you while I go and make you the best cup of tea you ever had.'

Bert knelt beside the lad. 'You seem to know this dog,' he said.

'It's Nell,' he replied. He kept patting the dog. 'Rob's dog. She's a clever dog. The best sheepdog in the Borders.'

'The dog certainly likes you, Jack,' Bert said.

Rob knelt down too. He looked the lad full in the face. In the stressed and worn features there was something he recognized. 'Jack? Is that your name?' he asked. 'Do I know you? Are you from round these parts?'

The boy didn't reply.

'It's *Jack*!' Millie exclaimed. 'He's the lad from the Otterby farm. We used to meet him on the hills at lambing time and at the sheepdog trials.'

'Jack the Lad,' the handcuffed soldier chimed in. 'Told you so. Should we put on a show to entertain the troops? We've got him and the dog. All we need now is a cow and a beanstalk and we're sorted.'

'You're all right there, Private Ames,' Bert quietened him.

'You reckon so?' The private held up his handcuffed wrist. 'I didn't think this would happen when I joined up.'

'We had to do that for your own protection. When we get to the hospital you'll get proper care.'

'Have they got magic beans there?' Private Ames grimaced. 'That's what we need. Magic beans. A cow, a beanstalk, and some magic beans.' He lapsed into mumbling to himself again. And all the while, Rob noted, he never once opened his eyes.

The nurse returned with two mugs of tea. She set one down in front of the handcuffed soldier and handed the other one to Jack. He looked at it suspiciously.

'I ain't drinking that,' he said. 'They put stuff in your tea, you know' – he partially covered his mouth with his hand as he spoke to Rob – 'to make you fight. Don't trust them. Don't trust any of them. Tell you lies. Say the wire's been cut. Land mines been cleared. *Advance! Enemy trenches destroyed! Advance! Advance! In line formation. Walk slowly. Shoulder to shoulder. Enemy trenches empty.* But they were waiting with machine guns to mow us down. Lies! Lies!'

Bert and the nurse glanced at each other. It was obvious that Jack was becoming agitated again.

'Would you like a plum-jam sandwich?' Millie took the teacloth off her basket and held it out.

Jack shook his head.

'I made them especially for my daddy in case he was on the train. Plum is his favourite jam and they're very tasty.'

'I'd like one,' the handcuffed soldier said. 'I can smell home-made jam and fresh bread.'

'My mummy made the jam and the bread, but I helped a lot,' Millie told him. She went over and guided his hands to the basket so he could take a sandwich.

'Oh, my,' said the private. 'That's the best food I've had for twelve months and a day.' He smacked his lips loudly with his eyes shut tight.

On sudden inspiration, Rob said, 'Don't forget to give Nell some.' He took a piece of bread and gave it to his dog.

As soon as he saw Nell eating the sandwich, Jack peered into the basket and selected one for himself. Then he lifted his mug and began to drink the tea. Bert and the nurse smiled in relief. The effect was almost immediate. Jack's eyelids drooped, and he slid sideways. The nurse rescued the mug from his limp fingers before it fell onto the floor. Bert went behind Jack and, placing his hands under his shoulders, pulled him along to the furthest part of the carriage. There he handcuffed his wrists to a metal pole.

Theresa Breslin

JILLY COOPER – Author

When I was a child, my favourite possession was a beautiful bay pony called Willow. My days were spent feeding her, grooming her so her coat shone like a conker, and riding her all over the moors. When I was eleven, it broke my heart that I was sent off to boarding school and didn't see my beloved Willow for thirteen weeks.

When I came home for Christmas, the most blissful moment was when she galloped down the field whickering with delighted surprise to see me again. I hardly left her side for the entire holidays. So imagine how much more terrible it would have been, if she'd been taken forcibly away to fight in a war.

A.M.D.G.

IN GRATEFUL AND REVERENT MEMORY

OF THE EMPIRE'S HORSES (SOME 375,000)

WHO FELL IN THE GREAT WAR (1914–18).

MOST OBEDIENTLY, AND OFTENMOST PAINFULLY,

THEY DIED.

'FAITHFUL UNTO DEATH NOT ONE OF THEM

IS FORGOTTEN BEFORE GOD'

EASTER 1926

*Inscription on the war memorial to horses
at St Jude on the Hill, Hampstead*

With the coming of the motor car and the bicycle, the horse population in England dwindled to such an extent that when war was declared in 1914, there was a huge dearth of suitable animals. Tillings, the London bus company, for example, who were already busy converting to horseless carriages, made a fortune selling a great many of their remaining horses to the army. Later, farmers in America, Argentina, Canada and Australia grew rich exporting horses to the Allies. But one of the cruellest ordeals for private owners in this country was when their family pets were called up. It seemed a kind of betrayal; you couldn't explain to a horse why he was being sent away. John Galsworthy expressed unashamed relief when his chestnut mare was rejected as unfit, and there exists a touching correspondence between some children and the War Office. Poppy, Lionel and Freda Hewlett wrote on 11 August 1914:

Dear Lord Kitchener,

We are writing for our pony, which we are very afraid may be taken for your army. Please spare her. Daddy says she is going to be a mother early next year, and is 17 years old. It would break our hearts to let her go. We have given 2 others and 3 of our family are now fighting for you in the Navy. Mother and all will do anything for you but do please let us keep old Betty, and send official word quickly before anyone comes.

Your troubled little Britishers
P., L. and Freda Hewlett

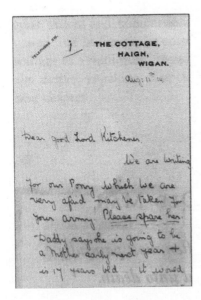
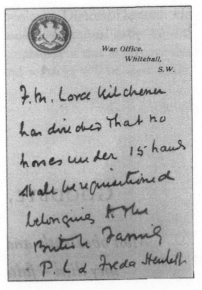

Happily Lord Kitchener's heart was touched. His private secretary wrote back by return of post, enclosing a note from the Colonel in charge of remounts: 'F.M. Lord Kitchener has decided that no horses under 15 hands shall be requisitioned belonging to the British family P., L. and Freda Hewlett.'

The overjoyed Hewletts replied:

To our good Lord Kitchener,

You are indeed kind to allow us to keep our dear old Betty. We met every post and hardly dared to hope you, who have so much to do, had had time to read our request, so little to you — so much to us . . . Always and ever your grateful British servants.

EOIN COLFER – Author

My most enduring childhood memories are those of waiting. I remember clearly lingering at windows and doors, watching for my father to return from wherever he might have been that day. I always had a pretext for being there – perhaps I had done well in school, or perhaps I was pre-empting a scolding by presenting my side of the story first – but really I was servicing that most primal of fears: that Daddy was never coming home. All children experience this fear to some degree or other, though we could never have expressed it aloud or even put a shape to it in our minds. But it's there, every day. Waiting.

I was one of the lucky ones in that my father always came home, most memorably with a little brother for me, which was a little anti-climactic as I had been expecting chips.

War stories tend to focus on the war itself, which is fair enough as the fighting is horrific and needs to be represented so that one day we may finally get the message and give up on war as a futile exercise, but there is another side to all conflict: the waiting. For the ones left behind, there is little to do but find a waiting spot and endure the torture of one's own imagination, and this is one of the themes of John Boyne's *Stay Where You Are and Then Leave*.

This wonderful book tells the story of nine-year-old London boy, Alfie, whose father went to war, leaving Alfie and his mum to play the dreaded waiting game. For Alfie there is no flood of relief at the end of every day with the sound of his father's boots clattering up to the front door. Alfie's father doesn't come home.

Determined to do his bit for the war effort, Alfie sets himself up as a shoeshine boy in King's Cross station, and during his shift one day he comes across a nugget of information that leads him to believe that his father is not quite as far away as he had thought.

Because this is a John Boyne book, I knew it would be beautiful and powerful but I had not expected to be so affected by Alfie's situation. I think there is something about Alfie that will bring any reader back to that time when they were nine years old and waited at the window for someone to come home. This is an agony that we don't usually see played out in First World War books, so it is important that people read this lovely book and see that the other side of war is represented. The ultimate horror of war is experienced by the soldiers in the trenches, but there is a quieter agony being endured by the loved ones left behind, and this is what we feel so keenly in *Stay Where You Are and Then Leave*.

FROM *STAY WHERE YOU ARE AND THEN LEAVE*

They said it would be over by Christmas, but four Christmases had already come and gone, a fifth was on the way, and the war showed no sign of coming to an end.

Alfie was nine years old now, and six mornings a week, his mum shook him awake when she was leaving for work. He still got a shock when he opened his eyes to see her standing there in the half-light, the white dress uniform of a Queen's Nurse gathered close around her neck and waist, the pleated cap settled neatly on her head as her tight blonde curls peeped out from underneath.

'Alfie,' she said, her face pale and tired from another night with so little sleep. 'Alfie, wake up. It's six o'clock.'

He groaned and rolled over, pulling the scratchy blanket over his head even though it meant his feet would stick out the other end, and tried to go back to sleep. He'd asked Margie for a new blanket, a longer and heavier one, but she said they couldn't afford one, that times were too tough now for unnecessary expenses. Alfie had been having a dream where he set sail for North Africa but his ship was destroyed in a storm. He'd managed to swim to a deserted island, where he was living off coconuts and fish and having any number of adventures. He always had this dream whenever he read *Robinson Crusoe*, and he was halfway through it again, for the fourth time. He'd stopped reading the night before just as Crusoe and Friday were watching the cannibals arrive in canoes with three prisoners ready for the pot. A big fight was about to break out; it was one of his favourite parts.

'Alfie, I don't have time for this,' said Margie. 'Wake up. I can't leave the house until you're out of bed.'

Her voice was unforgiving; one thing that Alfie noticed about the way his mother had changed over the last four years was how harsh she'd become. She never played with him any more – she was always too tired for that. She didn't read to him before bed; she couldn't, as she had to be back in the hospital by eight o'clock for the night shift. She talked about money all the time, or the lack of it. And she shouted at him for no reason and then looked as if she wanted to burst into tears for losing her temper.

'Alfie, please,' she said, pulling the sheets back so the cold got to him. 'You have to get up. Can't you just do this one thing for me?'

He knew he didn't have any choice, so he rolled over onto his back once again, opened his eyes, and gave a tremendous yawn and stretch before climbing slowly out of bed. Only when his feet were both planted on the floor did Margie stand up straight and nod, satisfied.

'Finally,' she said. 'Honestly, Alfie, I don't know why we have to go through this palaver every day. You're nine years old now. A little co-operation is all I ask for. Now get some breakfast into you, have a wash and go to school. I'll be back around two o'clock so I'll cook us something nice for our tea. What do you fancy?'

'Sausages, beans and chips,' said Alfie.

'Chance would be a fine thing,' said Margie, making a laughing sound that wasn't really a laugh at all. (She didn't laugh very much any more. Not in the way she used to when she said she'd run off with the postman.) 'Tripe and onions, I'm afraid. That's all we can afford.'

Alfie wondered why she asked what he fancied when it didn't seem to matter what his answer was. Still, he felt pleased that she would already be home when he finished school. It was usually much later before she got back from work.

'We'll have a bit of tea together,' she said, softening slightly. 'But I'm on a night shift again, I'm afraid, so you'll have to look after yourself this evening or you can pop over to Granny Summerfield's if you like. You won't get into any trouble, will you?'

Alfie shook his head. He'd tried talking her out of night shifts before but he never had any luck; she got a quarter extra in her pay packet when she worked after eight o'clock at night, and that quarter, she told him, could be the difference between them keeping a roof over their heads and not. He knew better than to bother trying any more. Margie stared at him for a moment, her hand reaching out and smoothing down his hair, and her expression changed a little. She didn't seem angry now. It was as if she was remembering the way things used to be. She sat down on the bed next to him and put her arm around his shoulders, and he cuddled into her, closing his eyes, feeling sleep returning.

After a moment he looked up and followed the direction of his mother's eyes until he found himself staring at the framed portrait of his father, Georgie, that stood on the table next to his bed. He wasn't wearing a soldier's uniform in it; instead he was standing in the yard at the dairy with a very young Alfie sitting on his shoulders, a big smile spread across his face, and Mr Asquith standing next to both of them, looking at the camera with an expression that suggested that this was an indignity he could do without. (Alfie always said that Mr Asquith was a very proud horse.) He couldn't remember when it had been taken but it had been standing on the table by his bed since the day Georgie had left for Aldershot Barracks four years earlier. Granny Summerfield had put it there that same evening.

'Oh Alfie,' said Margie, kissing him on his head as she stood up and made her way towards the door. 'I do my best for you. You know that, don't you?'

After she left for work, Alfie went downstairs, ran outside for the scoop that sat behind the back door, and filled it with ashes from the base of the kitchen range. Then he ran down to the privy at the end of the garden as quickly as he could, trying not to feel the ice in the air or spill any of the precious cinders. He hated going there first thing in the morning, particularly now, in late October, when it was still so dark and the air was so frosty, but there was no way around it.

It was freezing inside, seven different spiders and

something that looked like an overfed beetle crawled over his feet as he sat there, he could hear the scurrying of rats behind the woodwork, and he groaned when he remembered that he'd forgotten the squares of yesterday's newspaper that he meticulously cut up every night before going to bed – but fortunately Margie had taken them outside earlier, pinned a hole through their centre and hung them from a piece of string off the hook, so he didn't need to go back indoors.

When he had finished his business, he poured the ashes down the toilet and hoped that the compost heap around the back of the out-house – the worst place he had ever seen in his entire life – would not get clogged up again. It had happened a few months before, and Margie had to pay the night-soil men two shillings to clear it all away; afterwards, uncertain whether they would have enough money for the rent, she had sat down in the broken armchair in front of the fireplace and cried her eyes out, whispering Georgie's name under her breath over and over again as if he might be able to come back and save them from possible eviction.

Alfie ran back inside, washed his hands and sat down at the kitchen table, where Margie had cut two slices of bread for him and left them on a plate next to a small scraping of butter and, to his astonishment, a tiny pot of jam with a muslin lid held in place by a piece of string. Alfie stared at it and blinked a couple of times. It had been months since he'd tasted jam. He picked it up and read the label. It was handwritten and contained only one word, written with a thick black pen.

Gooseberry.

Sometimes the parents of the soldiers in the hospital brought in a little something for the Queen's Nurses, and when they did, it was usually a treat like this: something they'd made themselves from the fruit they grew in their gardens or allotments. That must have been where Margie had got it. Alfie wondered whether his mother had eaten some herself or whether she'd kept it specially for him. He stood up and went over to the sink, where his mother's breakfast things were sitting, still unwashed, a small pool of cold brown tea sitting at the base of her mug. In the old days, before the war, Margie would never have left things like this; she would have rinsed them out and turned them upside down on the draining board for Georgie to dry later. He picked up the plate and examined it. There were a few crumbs on the side and a trace of condensation from where the heat of the toast had clashed with the coldness of the porcelain. He looked at the knife. It was almost clean. He gave it a sniff. It didn't smell of butter and there wasn't a trace of jam on it. If she'd used any, it would have left a bit behind.

She'd saved it all for him.

Alfie filled the kettle, put it on the range, threw a few sticks on top of the still-red embers inside and waited for the whistle before making himself a cup of tea. He always felt like a grown-up waiting for the leaves to brew. He didn't much like the taste of it, but it made him feel important to sit at the table in the morning with a steaming mug and a slice of toast before him, the newspaper propped up against the milk jug. It was how Georgie had always done things. Before he went away.

Charlie Slipton from number twenty-one didn't deliver the papers any more. He'd left for the war in 1917 and been killed a few months later. Alfie had written the name of the place where he died in his notebook but still couldn't pronounce it correctly. *Passchendaele*. Now the papers were delivered by Charlie's youngest brother, Jack, who had just turned ten and never spoke to anyone. Alfie had tried to make friends with him but eventually gave up when it became clear that he preferred to be left alone.

Looking at the newspaper now made him think of that horrible day a year ago when they'd heard about Charlie's death. It was a Sunday morning, so both he and Margie had been at home when there was a knock at the door. Margie, who had been baking bread, looked up in surprise, running the back of her hand against her forehead and leaving a white streak of flour behind. They didn't have many callers. Granny Summerfield had her own key and usually came straight in without so much as a by-your-leave. Old Bill next door always did a sort of *rat-a-tat-tat* on the woodwork so they'd know it was him. And of course Mr Janáček and Kalena had been taken away to the Isle of Man. Alfie didn't like to think about what had happened to them there.

'Who do you think that is?' asked Margie, rinsing her hands in the sink before walking into the hallway and standing before the door for a moment as if she might be able to see straight through to the other side. Alfie followed her, and after a moment she stepped forward, reached for the latch and opened it.

There were two men standing outside, both wearing military uniforms. One was quite old with a grey moustache, a pair of spectacles and dark blue eyes. He wore a very fine pair of leather gloves, which he was in the process of removing when the door was opened. The other man was much younger and had cut himself shaving that morning; Alfie could see a bead of blood clotted on his cheek. He had bright red hair that stuck out at all angles and looked as if it would put up a good fight against any brush that tried to tame it. Alfie stared at him in wonder. He'd never seen hair that red before, not even on Mr

Carstairs, his teacher at Damley Road School, who everybody called 'Ginger' even though his hair was really more like a burned orange.

'Don't,' said Margie, holding onto the front door as she stared at the two men, her hand clutching the frame tightly. Alfie saw how white her knuckles became as she gripped it. *'Don't,'* she repeated, much louder this time, and Alfie frowned, wondering what she could possibly mean by this single word.

'Mrs Slipton?' said the older man, the one with the moustache, as the redhead stood to his full height and looked over Margie's shoulder to lock eyes with Alfie. His expression turned to one of sorrow when he saw the boy, and he bit his lip and looked away.

'What?' asked Margie, her voice rising in surprise at being addressed by the wrong name. Alfie stepped forward beside his mum now, and he noticed all the doors opening on the opposite side of the street and the women coming out and putting their hands to their faces. The curtain at number eleven twitched, and he could see Granny Summerfield staring out, her hands pressed to the side of her head. Mr Asquith trotted by with young Henry Lyons on the bench-seat. Henry couldn't fill a milk jug to save his life; everyone said so. He'd start pouring and half the churn would end up on the side of the road. But the dairy needed a delivery man, and Henry was deaf so couldn't go to war. Alfie was sure that Mr Asquith stared in his direction as he passed, looking over the boy's shoulder in search of his true master.

'Mrs Slipton, I'm Sergeant Malley,' said the man. 'This is Lieutenant Hobton. May we come in for a moment?'

'No,' said Margie.

'Mrs Slipton, please,' he replied in a resigned tone, as if he was accustomed to this type of response. 'If we could just come in and sit down, then—'

'You've got the wrong house,' said Margie, her words catching in her throat, and she almost stumbled before putting her hand on Alfie's shoulder to steady herself. 'Oh my God, you've got the wrong house. How can you do that? This is number twelve. You want number twenty-one. You've got the numbers backwards.'

The older man stared at her for a moment; then his expression changed to one of utter dismay as the redhead pulled a piece of paper from his inside pocket and ran his eyes across it quickly.

'Sarge,' he said, holding the paper out and pointing at something.

The sergeant's lip curled up in fury and he glared at the younger man as if he wanted to hit him. 'What's wrong with you, Hobton?' he hissed. 'Can't you read? Can't you check before we knock on a door?' He turned back then and looked at Margie and Alfie, shaking his head. 'I'm sorry,' he said. 'I'm so very, very sorry.'

And with that the two men turned round but remained on the street, looking left and right, their eyes scanning the numbers on the doors before turning in the direction of Mr Janáček's sweet shop, where the windows were still boarded up from when they'd been smashed a couple of years before and the three words painted in white remained.

No Spies Here!

Margie stepped back into the hall, gasping, but Alfie stayed in the doorway. He watched as the two soldiers made their way slowly along the street. Every door was open now. And outside every door stood a wife or a mother. Some were crying. Some were praying. Some were shaking their heads, hoping that

the men wouldn't stop before them. And every time Sergeant
Malley and Lieutenant Hobton passed one of the houses, the
woman at the door blessed herself and ran inside, slamming it
behind her and putting the latch on in case the two men changed
their minds and came back.

Finally they stopped at number twenty-one, where Charlie's
mother, Mrs Slipton, was standing. Alfie couldn't hear what
she was saying but he could see her crying, trying to push the
soldiers away. She reached out with both hands and slapped
Redhead across the face, but somehow he didn't seem to mind.
The older man reached forward and whispered something to
her, and then they went inside and stayed there, and Alfie
found himself alone on the street again. Everyone else was
indoors, counting their lucky stars that the two soldiers hadn't
stopped at their door.

Later that day, Alfie heard that Charlie Slipton had been
killed and he remembered the afternoon when Charlie had
thrown a stone at his head for no reason whatsoever. He
wasn't sure how he was supposed to feel. That was the thing
about the war, he realized. It made everything so confusing.

Alfie didn't read much of the *Daily Mirror* but he liked
to look at the headlines, and he picked it up now to see what
was going on in the world. More news about the Marne; there
was always something going on there. Details of casualties and
fatalities from a place called Amiens. A report on a speech by
the Prime Minister, Mr Lloyd George, who Alfie was sick of
reading about because he gave speeches every day.

And then, finally, he did what he always did in the morning.
He turned to page four to read the numbers. The number of
deaths on our side. The number of deaths on their side. The
number of wounded. The number missing in action. But there

was only one number that Alfie really cared about: 14278. His dad's number. The number they'd assigned him when he signed up.

He ran his finger along the list.

14143, Smith, D., Royal Fusiliers
14275, Dempster, C. K., Gloucestershire Regiment
15496, Wallaby, A., Seaforth Highlanders
15700, Crosston, J., Sherwood Foresters (Notts &
Derby Regiment)

He breathed a sigh of relief and put the paper down, sipping his tea, trying to think of something else.

John Boyne

ANNE HARVEY – Writer, biographer and actress

Eleanor Farjeon, one of the most famous twentieth-century children's writers, wrote many novels, books of short stories, plays and poetry for adults. She also wrote the lyrics for the hymn 'Morning Has Broken', and an award in her name is presented annually for excellence in the world of children's literature.

Eleanor always said that the greatest love and most special friendship in her life was with the writer Edward Thomas, whom she first met in a café in the Strand, London, in 1912. The two instantly liked each other, met frequently, and in between wrote to each other. Eleanor became friends with his wife, and close to his three children, and when he began writing poetry, typed his poems for him.

Edward Thomas burned many letters before he went to France as a soldier with the Artists Rifles, but 200 letters that he sent to Eleanor form her memoir *Edward Thomas: The Last Four Years*. The Book unfolds important moments in their friendship. Eleanor was one of the first people to ask him: 'Haven't you ever written poetry, Edward?' His answer was 'Me? I couldn't write a poem to save my life'!

She writes that later, she asked him why he had joined the army, and what he was fignting for:

'He stopped and picked up a pinch of earth. "Literally for this." He crumbled it between finger and thumb and let it fall. '

In that action he had expressed to her his love for his country felt by so many men who subsequently joined the army.

Eleanor Farjeon was known for her generous present-giving to friends and family, and she ordered, from the London store Fortnum and Mason, a box of Cox's Orange Pippins and a silver-wrapped Easter egg to be sent to Edward in France, for Easter Sunday – 8 April 1917.

Edward Thomas was killed during the Battle of Arras on Easter Monday – 9 April 1917 – and Eleanor was puzzled to receive a letter from him after this, dated 3 April – six days *before* the battle. 'Edward's last letter of all came after his death. It was begun in ink, six days before the battle, and finished in pencil five days later . . .'

April 3
My dear Eleanor. I didn't discover the Egg till Easter Monday because I was taking apples out from a corner I had nibbled out. So now I must write again to thank you for an Easter Egg. It was such a lovely morning Easter Monday . . .

He also tells her:

Well, this is the eve and a beautiful sunny day after a night of cold and snow . . .

And after describing the weather, and the concern that the good weather might also help the enemy, he explains how he has been strengthening the dug-out and keeping it free from *drip-drip*. He ends with:

So goodbye. May I have a letter before long. Yours ever, Edward Thomas.

Eleanor realized that he had been confused over dates, but included this strange happening in the most moving of the sonnets she wrote for him.

EASTER MONDAY

(In Memoriam E.T.)

In the last letter that I had from France
You thanked me for the silver Easter egg
Which I had hidden in the box of apples
You liked to munch beyond all other fruit.
You found the egg the Monday before Easter,
And said, 'I will praise Easter Monday now –
It was such a lovely morning.' Then you spoke
Of the coming battle and said, 'This is the eve.
Goodbye. And may I have a letter soon.'

That Easter Monday was a day for praise,
It was such a lovely morning. In our garden
We sowed our earliest seeds, and in the orchard
The apple-bud was ripe. It was the eve.
There are three letters that you will not get.

Eleanor Farjeon

DAME GAIL REBUCK – Chair of Penguin Random House UK

Seamus Heaney's 'heartbreakingly prescient' poem 'In a Field', inspired by Edward Thomas's 1916 poem 'As the team's head-brass', was possibly the last poem Heaney wrote before he died on 30 August 2013.

'As the team's head-brass', written a year before Thomas died in 1917, looks at how the human experience of war invaded the English countryside. 'In a Field' was commissioned by the above-quoted Carol Ann Duffy, for a memorial anthology to mark the centenary of the First World War. Set in a rural landscape, it tells of a demobbed soldier, returning to the land.

Both poems look at the human cost of war set against an enduring landscape.

I chose them because the secret to remembering and honouring the past is to constantly re-imagine it for new generations.

In a Field

And there I was in the middle of a field,
The furrows once called 'scores' still with their gloss,
The tractor with its hoisted plough just gone

Snarling at an unexpected speed
Out on the road. Last of the jobs,
The windings had been ploughed, furrows turned

Three ply or four round each of the four sides
Of the breathing land, to mark it off
And out. Within that boundary now

Step the fleshy earth and follow
The long healed footprints of one who arrived
From nowhere, unfamiliar and de-mobbed,

In buttoned khaki and buffed army boots,
Bruising the turned-up acres of our back field
To stumble from the windings' magic ring

And take me by a hand to lead me back
Through the same old gate into the yard
Where everyone has suddenly appeared,
All standing waiting.

Seamus Heaney

AS THE TEAM'S HEAD-BRASS

As the team's head-brass flashed out on the turn
The lovers disappeared into the wood.
I sat among the boughs of the fallen elm
That strewed an angle of the fallow, and
Watched the plough narrowing a yellow square
Of charlock. Every time the horses turned
Instead of treading me down, the ploughman leaned
Upon the handles to say or ask a word,
About the weather, next about the war.

Scraping the share he faced towards the wood,
And screwed along the furrow till the brass flashed
Once more.
The blizzard felled the elm whose crest
I sat in, by a woodpecker's round hole,
The ploughman said. 'When will they take it away?'
'When the war's over.' So the talk began –
One minute and an interval of ten,
A minute more and the same interval.
'Have you been out?' 'No.' 'And don't want to, perhaps?'
'If I could only come back again, I should.
I could spare an arm. I shouldn't want to lose
A leg. If I should lose my head, why, so,
I should want nothing more . . . Have many gone
From here?' 'Yes.' 'Many lost?' 'Yes: a good few.
Only two teams work on the farm this year.
One of my mates is dead. The second day
In France they killed him. It was back in March,
The very night of the blizzard, too. Now if
He had stayed here we should have moved the tree.'
'And I should not have sat here. Everything
Would have been different. For it would have been
Another world.' 'Ay, and a better, though
If we could see all all might seem good.' Then
The lovers came out of the wood again:
The horses started and for the last time
I watched the clods crumble and topple over
After the ploughshare and the stumbling team.

Edward Thomas

ALAN TITCHMARSH – Horticulturalist, broadcaster and author

As far back as I can remember I have been interested in nature and things that grow.

I was born and spent my childhood in the Yorkshire Dales, where the moors, the woods and the river became a favourite playground.

I was not particularly good at school, and absolutely useless at maths and physics – both were a complete puzzle to me. I felt stupid at not being able to grasp what my teachers were doing their best to explain. It seemed so simple to them, and yet so completely baffling to me. But I loved being outdoors and learning about flowers. I found I could make seeds grow from a packet bought in Woolworths, and get cuttings that I would snip from pot plants to put out roots and grow into new ones. Plants and animals seemed far more realistic and straightforward to me than equations and verbs. I joined the Wharfedale Naturalists at the age of eight – its youngest member.

It was much later in my life that I came across a poem by Edward Thomas, who was killed in the First World War. Thomas lived not far from where I live now, in Hampshire. Like Yorkshire, Hampshire has wonderful countryside: rolling hills, valleys through which run crystal-clear rivers, and chalk downs literally smothered in wild flowers in spring and summer.

These were things that Edward Thomas loved. Things that were a part of his everyday life. Things that he noticed and cherished. In that respect he was just like me.

I left school at fifteen and became a gardener in a nursery filled with old greenhouses and sheds. Edward Thomas's poem

'Tall Nettles' has always struck a chord with me. Here was a man – like so many others in that dreadful war – who was, at heart, a countryman; an observant man, sensitive to the ways of nature, who found himself at the mercy of human nature.

When I think about the dreadful tragedy of the Great War, the loss of life – both human and animal, for horses were the main form of transport in those days – I think too of the things the men, and horses, left behind at home. Many of them would have been farmers and growers, gardeners and gamekeepers, men of the countryside. 'Tall Nettles' reminds me that, for them, beyond the dreadful conflict and the sea of mud that was the Battle of the Somme, there was a countryside they felt worth fighting for.

Tall Nettles

Tall nettles cover up, as they have done
These many springs, the rusty harrow, the plough
Long worn out, and the roller made of stone:
Only the elm butt tops the nettles now.

This corner of the farmyard I like most:
As well as any bloom upon a flower
I like the dust on the nettles, never lost
Except to prove the sweetness of a shower.

Edward Thomas

JOANNA LUMLEY – Actress

GV RI

HE whom this scroll commemorates was numbered among those who, at the call of King and Country, left all that was dear to them, endured hardness, faced danger, and finally passed out of the sight of men by the path of duty and self-sacrifice, giving up their own lives that others might live in freedom. Let those who come after see to it that his name be not forgotten.

Pte (short for Private) William James Martin,
Devonshire Regiment

I find this extremely moving and dignified – and poignant, as Rudyard Kipling, who wrote this short piece for the commemorative scrolls sent to the families of soldiers who would never return, was to lose his own beloved son, from whose death he never fully recovered. He hunted in vain for the site of his son's grave or remains, haunted by guilt, as he had pulled strings to get the boy accepted into the army even though his eyesight was very poor.

I love the strange, quiet solace in the phrase 'Finally passed out of the sight of men . . .' It seems to imply that although mortals cannot see them any more, other kindly eyes are watching them and taking care of them in the mystery that is death. It is carefully written to comfort people of any religion or of none, and to honour the life and sacrifice of each young soul.

This citation was presented on a handsome scroll with the royal crest of King George V above in black, his initials, GV RI – George V, *Rex Imperator* (King Emperor) – with the snarling lion and the prancing unicorn, the mottoes *Dieu et Mon Droit* (God and My Right) and *Honi soit qui mal y pense* (Shame on him who thinks evil of it) written on the garlanding ribbons.

The soldier's name was written in red, as if in blood, at the bottom, with his regiment below – for instance:

Pte [short for Private] William James Martin,
Devonshire Regiment

How many grieving families received this scroll! It may have come as a small comfort, especially for those little children who then grew up without a father; but if you listen closely, you can still hear the cries of sorrow echoing around the world in today's conflicts.

JENNY AGUTTER – Actress

My only connection with the First World War is through my grandfather, Frank Agutter.

I never spoke with him about it; I was very young and knew nothing about the two world wars. My parents had been children in the Second World War and made sure my brother and I were unaffected by all that had troubled them growing up.

I knew my grandfather as a gentle, elderly man who taught me about trees, helping me recognize the shapes of the leaves, the bark and the way the trees grew. He was a good amateur watercolour artist, inspiring in me an interest in drawing and painting. I still have his small tin paintbox and brushes.

Frank Agutter was with the West Yorkshire Regiment and fought at the Somme, where he became a prisoner of war. He survived, and on his release he was told to walk home. That was as much as he would say to his family about what he had experienced.

My great-grandmother must have often thought she would never see her son again. Like so many, she waited and hoped, and felt extraordinarily lucky when he did come back.

We still have the First World War medals my grandfather received (see over). They were given to all soldiers who took part in the war. My father said they were referred to as Pip Squeak and Wilfred!

This poem of J. C. Squire's tells a personal story of loss. When it was written, the bulldog was representative of British courage, but

in this poem she is a loved pet – Mamie, an animal who will wait patiently, but will never understand that she is waiting in vain; that her friend Willy will never return. J. C. Squire talks to Mamie about the memories that occupy his mind and the terrible feeling of loss that he will always know.

TO A BULLDOG

We shan't see Willy any more, Mamie,
He won't be coming any more:
He came back once and again and again,
But he won't get leave any more.

We looked from the window and there was his cab,
And we ran downstairs like a streak,
And he said, 'Hullo, you bad dog,'
    and you crouched to the floor,
Paralysed to hear him speak.

And then let fly at his face and his chest
Till I had to hold you down,
While he took off his cap and his gloves and his coat,
And his bag and his thonged Sam Browne.

We went upstairs to the studio,
The three of us, just as of old,
And you lay down and I sat and talked to him
As round the room he strolled.

Here in the room where, years ago
Before the old life stopped,
He worked all day with his slippers and his pipe,
He would pick up the threads he'd dropped,

Fondling all the drawings he had left behind,
Glad to find them all still the same,
And opening the cupboards to look at his belongings
. . . Every time he came.

But now I know what a dog doesn't know,
Though you'll thrust your head on my knee,
And try to draw me from the absent-mindedness
That you find so dull in me.

And all your life, you will never know
What I wouldn't tell you even if I could,
That the last time we waved him away
Willy went for good.

But sometimes as you lie on the hearthrug
Sleeping in the warmth of the stove,
Even through your muddled old canine brain
Shapes from the past may rove.

You'll scarcely remember, even in a dream,
How we brought home a silly little pup,
With a big square head and little crooked legs
That could scarcely bear him up,

But your tail will tap at the memory
Of a man whose friend you were,
Who was always kind though he called you a naughty dog
When he found you in his chair;

Who'd make you face a reproving finger
And solemnly lecture you
Till your head hung downwards and you looked very
sheepish:
And you'll dream of your triumphs too,

Of summer evening chases in the garden
When you dodged us all about with a bone:
We were three boys, and you were the cleverest,
But now we're two alone.

When summer comes again,
And the long sunsets fade,
We shall have to go on playing the feeble game for two
That since the war we've played.

And though you run expectant as you always do
To the uniforms we meet,
You'll never find Willy among all the soldiers
In even the longest street,

Nor in any crowd; yet, strange and bitter thought,
Even now were the old words said,
If I tried the old trick and said, 'Where's Willy?'
You would quiver and lift your head,

And your brown eyes would look to ask if I was serious
And wait for the word to spring.
Sleep undisturbed: I shan't say that again,
You innocent old thing.

I must sit, not speaking, on the sofa,
While you lie asleep on the floor;
For he's suffered a thing that dogs couldn't dream of,
And he won't be coming here any more.

J. C. Squire

SANDI TOKSVIG – Writer, presenter, comedian, actress and producer

This was a song written in 1914 which became a big hit in the United States. America did not enter the First World War until 6 April 1917. Before then there were many Americans who thought the war was wrong. Many of them were 'pacifists', which is what we call people who are against war and violence; who believe that disputes should be settled through talking, not fighting. This song represented those ideas, and it's important to remember that there have always been voices in favour of peace. I like it because it reminds us that every soldier, no matter where they come from, is someone's child.

It was unusual for a war song to give a mother's perspective. Women were not able to vote in 1914, and those who fought for women's rights at the time also liked this song. They were called 'suffragettes', and they joined with the pacifists in singing these words.

I hope I would have been both a suffragette and a pacifist. The fact is, there would be no wars in the world if every mother stood up and refused to allow her boy to fight.

I Didn't Raise My Boy to Be a Soldier

Ten million soldiers to the war have gone,
Who may never return again.
Ten million mothers' hearts must break
For the ones who died in vain.
Head bowed down in sorrow
In her lonely years,
I heard a mother murmur thru' her tears:

I didn't raise my boy to be a soldier,
I brought him up to be my pride and joy.
Who dares to place a musket on his shoulder,
To shoot some other mother's darling boy?
Let nations arbitrate their future troubles,
It's time to lay the sword and gun away.
There'd be no war today,
If mothers all would say,
'I didn't raise my boy to be a soldier.'

What victory can cheer a mother's heart,
When she looks at her blighted home?
What victory can bring her back
All she cared to call her own?
Let each mother answer
In the years to be,
Remember that my boy belongs to me!

Lyrics by Alfred Bryan; music by Al Piantadosi

LAURA DOCKRILL – Writer, performance poet and illustrator

I never actively search for literature. I enjoy reading and writing because it is a natural and relaxing way for me to spend time, as well as my job. Which is writing and reading. I am certain it would squeeze the luxury and enjoyment out of it if it ever became forced.

I like writing, in all its forms, to find me; however, this piece didn't find me. I found myself more ... being ... chased by it, summoned ... caught and then strangled. There is something so urgent and arresting about the whole piece. It feels truly impatient, frustrated – like a diary entry, almost, but also a bit wanting the whole world to read it. For me, for its age, this is one of the most striking, brave and remarkable pieces of text I have come across. Apart from being stunningly written, attacked appropriately, executed with personality and written with such a strong voice, the piece is perfectly paced and balanced, moving and scratchy. It is angry yet passive, bitter yet positive, hopeful yet regretful. Annoyed. *Fed up*. It's how my mates and I sound when we are whining, but then it's got this gravity behind it. A warmth.

We have an extended knowledge of the war. A collection of stuff thrust into our faces that over time has left us in its wake with a very blurry, mixed and confusing collage: some facts from school; a crossover in history and English, overlapping into geography sometimes, art and drama. It is patchy and always changing. We visit museums; we see images, read letters. The media fills in the gaps with the help from our imaginations, but that is merged with cinematic interpretations. The war for my younger brother probably looks like a scene from *Call of Duty*, where he can lift up a digital computerized barrel and find himself a first-aid pack. And then there's what my beloved nanna talks to me about, sitting in her chair in her furry slippers, sipping on a teacup and saucer of chalky coffee, the photograph of her father, proud in uniform, by her side. That helps too.

But rarely do we hear a voice. A woman's voice. A woman voice *wanting*. Removed but also so clinging. And how I never came across this at school, *a girls' school*, is beyond me. Because it says something more personal and immediately political about a war than I have previously been exposed to. I would only have to read: 'In a trench you are sitting, while I am knitting,' or, my favourite stanza:

> Was there a scrap or ploy in which you, the boy,
>   Could better me? You could not climb higher,
> Ride straighter, run as quick (and to smoke made you sick)
> . . . But I sit here, and you're under fire.

to gain a sense of the humans who lived this. I would have identified on a deeper level – the anxiety, the frustration, the loss, the heartache – as someone who has a brother and would have felt exactly the same.

Many Sisters to Many Brothers

When we fought campaigns (in the long Christmas rains)
    With soldiers spread in troops on the floor,
I shot as straight as you, my losses were as few,
    My victories as many, or more.
And when in naval battle, amid cannon's rattle,
    Fleet met fleet in the bath,
My cruisers were as trim, my battleships as grim,
    My submarines cut as swift a path.
Or, when it rained too long, and the strength of the strong
    Surged up and broke a way with blows,
I was as fit and keen, my fists hit as clean,
    Your black eye matched my bleeding nose.
Was there a scrap or ploy in which you, the boy,
    Could better me? You could not climb higher,
Ride straighter, run as quick (and to smoke made you sick)
. . . But I sit here, and you're under fire.

Oh, it's you that have the luck, out there in blood and
muck:
    You were born beneath a kindly star;
All we dreamt, I and you, you can really go and do,
    And I can't, the way things are.
In a trench you are sitting, while I am knitting
    A hopeless sock that never gets done.
Well, here's luck, my dear; – and you've got it, no fear;
    But for me . . . a war is poor fun.

Rose Macaulay

VIRGINIA MCKENNA – Actress, author and wildlife campaigner

Why is it that some poems make you catch your breath? Bring sudden tears? This one does that for me. Each time I read it. Perhaps it defines, describes, in such a poignant, piercing way, that there really is no space between the old and the young. Everyone has a mother, as Teresa Hooley says, and the old veteran was once the child she holds on her knee so tenderly, and with such fearful anticipation of what might lie ahead.

There have been many poems written about war and death and suffering. But this one, in its heart-breaking simplicity, touches my heart beyond imagining.

A War Film

I saw,
With a catch of the breath and the heart's uplifting,
Sorrow and pride,
the 'week's great draw' –
The Mons Retreat;
The 'Old Contemptibles' who fought, and died,
The horror and the anguish and the glory.

As in a dream,
Still hearing machine-guns rattle and shells scream,

I came out into the street.
When the day was done,
My little son
Wondered at bath-time why I kissed him so,
Naked upon my knee.
How could he know
The sudden terror that assaulted me? . . .
The body I had borne
Nine moons beneath my heart,
A part of me . . .
If, someday,
It should be taken away
To war. Tortured. Torn.
Slain.
Rotting in No Man's Land, out in the rain –
My little son . . .
Yet all those men had mothers, every one.

How should he know
Why I kissed and kissed and kissed him, crooning his
name?
He thought that I was daft.
He thought it was a game,
And laughed, and laughed.

Teresa Hooley

KATE MOSSE – Novelist and playwright

At the time of the First World War, Rudyard Kipling was a fabulously successful and popular British writer of short stories and adventure novels for children, such as *The Jungle Book*, *Kim* and the *Just So Stories*. In 1907 he was awarded the Nobel Prize for Literature, the first English writer ever to be honoured in this way, and was invited to be the Poet Laureate (though he turned that down!). But Kipling was also a dazzling and imaginative poet, admired for his rhythm and metre, for his outstanding ability to tell a story in verse and for his ability to write about huge issues – war, empire, relationships between people from different parts of the world, faith – and also about very personal emotions.

This poem is a mixture of both. Kipling wrote it after the death of his beloved and only son John (known as Jack) at the Battle of Loos in September 1915. Jack was only eighteen and had been in the British Army for just two weeks when he was reported injured and missing in action. Kipling and his wife went to France and searched desperately, urgently, for their son in local villages and field hospitals. They never found him or discovered what had happened to him. Jack's name appears on the Loos Memorial, one of 20,000 young men who have no known grave. Later, Kipling became involved with the War Graves Commission, no doubt in part as a way to cope with his grief.

The Battle of Loos took place between 25 September and 14 October 1915, and was one of the largest British-French offensives of the First World War. It was also the first time the British Army used poison gas.

In this beautiful, short poem, Kipling doesn't write directly of his own experience, but rather imagines another grieving father seeking news of his missing son, perhaps drowned at sea. The emotions are of loss and courage, and the imagery is nautical – the wind and the waves, rather than the mud and gas of the Western Front – but the poem stands as poignant and permanent a memorial as anything built of stone or marble.

MY BOY JACK

'Have you news of my boy Jack?'
    Not this tide.
'When d'you think that he'll come back?'
    Not with this wind blowing, and this tide.

'Has any one else had word of him?'
    Not this tide.
For what is sunk will hardly swim,
    Not with this wind blowing, and this tide.

'Oh, dear, what comfort can I find?'
    None this tide,
    Nor any tide,
Except he did not shame his kind –
    Not even with that wind blowing, and that tide.

Then hold your head up all the more,
    This tide,
    And every tide;
Because he was the son you bore,
    And gave to that wind blowing and that tide!

Rudyard Kipling

SHIRLEY HUGHES – Author and illustrator

John Singer Sargent's terrifying picture of a staggering line of First World War soldiers who had been blinded in a gas attack haunted me as a child. The Great War, as it was called then, cast a long and terrible shadow over our cosy, protected early childhood before the Second World War came to shatter it. To us it was the equivalent of the Holocaust. Many fathers of my school friends had served in it; some had returned without an arm or a leg, or silently struggling with some deep, unhealed scar of the mind.

Yet the imagery of that war fascinated me. There was little explicit horror. In the illustrated magazines that covered the events, old copies of which still lay about, many of the scenes were drawn by war artists rather than photographed. They concentrated on upbeat morale-boosting pictures for the folks at home. The coverage was highly censored. What came to us, in the early 1930s, was a kind of hushed, overwhelming sadness; a terrible thing, better not talked about but always there. During the two minutes of silence on Armistice Day everything, even the traffic in the streets, stopped as people snapped to attention with bowed heads.

The imagery of war memorials was everywhere. There was hardly a village in the British Isles without one. There were the more elaborate ones – monuments with noble memoirs, bandaged heads lifted up heroically over a dead comrade – or a more generalized personification of grief: a mourning Niobe in full Art Nouveau kitsch drapery. Some, by far the most moving, were simply tablets with lists of names, in post offices, in railway stations, in offices, shops and town halls, of local men who had given their lives.

One realistic depiction, which I had never actually seen but knew of from reproduction, was C. Sargeant Jagger's life-size bronzes of real gunners on the Royal Artillery Memorial at Hyde Park Corner. One is dead, covered with a cape. The others stand; their steadfast and uncharismatic poses Turn to page 90 to see one of Jagger's memorials. make a heart-stopping impact. These are real soldiers and therefore so much more heroic.

Even during the Second World War the images of war we saw in newsreels and newspapers were heavily censored. It was thought that the reality would depress morale. Now we see the cruelty and barbarity of war almost daily on television. This saturation is, I imagine, why the most telling and publicly acclaimed monuments to the dead of recent wars are those in which unbearable grief is expressed in stark, abstract simplicity, like Maya Ying Lin's Vietnam Veterans Memorial in Washington. The wall of black Indian granite on which the names are carved – over 58,000 of them – is so highly Turn to the plate section in the middle of the book to see *Gassed* in colour polished that the living, filing silently past, are reflected in it like ghosts.

JON SNOW – Journalist

I first had Rupert Brooke's emblematic poem 'The Soldier' read to me on Remembrance Sunday when I was eight years old. I was a chorister at Winchester Cathedral, and that day was my first awakening to the scale of the war that my parents and teachers had lived through.

There was a sombre romance in Brooke's tragic death of a fever in 1915 on his way to the Gallipoli landings. The discovery that he was only twenty-eight when he died, and yet had written so tellingly of his understanding of death and burial in a foreign field, seized my innocent heart.

As boys, we revisited that poem often. Winchester Cathedral was, and remains, festooned with memorials to thousands who died in war in foreign fields. Hence Brooke's thoughts had a poignant resonance as we trooped in cassocks and surplices around the transepts of that exceptional building.

In later life, 'The Soldier' and the memory of Brooke have given me a particular perspective on modern wars that I have had to report. Looking at the poem now, I'm struck that a not particularly bright small boy of eight found so much within its lines.

> The Gallipoli landings took place between 25 April 1915 and 9 January 1918. The British attacked Turkish fortresses (Turkey was in alliance with Germany) in the hope of ending their participation in the war. Instead, the campaign was a very bloody and public failure.

THE SOLDIER

If I should die, think only this of me:
    That there's some corner of a foreign field
That is for ever England. There shall be
    In that rich earth a richer dust concealed;
A dust whom England bore, shaped, made aware,
    Gave, once, her flowers to love, her ways to roam,
A body of England's, breathing English air,
    Washed by the rivers, blest by suns of home.

And think, this heart, all evil shed away,
    A pulse in the eternal mind, no less
    Gives somewhere back the thoughts by England given;
Her sights and sounds; dreams happy as her day;
    And laughter, learnt of friends; and gentleness,
    In hearts at peace, under an English heaven.

Rupert Brooke

SIR ANDREW MOTION – Poet

MISSING

When my grandfather (my father's father) died in 1980 he left me his desk – a dark, heavy, Victorian partner's desk, far too wide for the terraced house I lived in then, and for every house I've lived in since. I liked it but it belonged to a different age; it implied expectations I could never share.

But never mind. In the middle drawer, put there by the last and nicest of my grandfather's girlfriends, was the photograph album he had kept for the first half of his life – from his schooldays in the early 1900s through to the 1950s. This was a much more interesting thing to inherit, a collection of pictures in which difference became a fascination, not a problem.

Most absorbing of all were the pictures he had taken with some kind of Box Brownie immediately after the outbreak of war in August 1914. Tiny deckle-edged things, small enough to make me lean forward and screw up my eyes. To hold my breath so nothing escaped me. There he was sitting beside his father on the steps of their house near Edgehill: my great-grandfather slouched, weary and wary; my grandfather perky and upright in his brand-new uniform. Then in the same uniform, the uniform of the Warwickshire Yeomanry, and this time learning how to dig trenches – in Newbury of all places. Then not him but his beautiful chestnut hunter, the horse he took with him when he was posted to Alexandria, and which drowned when its transport ship was sunk by a torpedo. Then him again: ashore now, on the Egyptian coast where he was billeted. In a village called Glymenopoulo.

But what's he doing there? Not training – or not in the pictures, anyway. Having fun. Strolling along the sand with a girl on his arm, shielding her from the sun with a pale silk parasol. The girl's wearing a black bathing costume, and so is he by the look of it – but it's hard to see properly, the pictures are so small, and so dark. Yes, her hair is wet and so is his. They've been swimming together; now they're sauntering back to a bar for a drink, for a bite of lunch, for some supper.

And what's the date? 'Summer 1915'. That's during the Gallipoli landings, when thousands of Allied troops were killed and thousands more were invalided out – many to Alexandria. On the next page of the album I can see the ships, a procession of them scattered over the shining sea like dots and dashes in a morse code message. And on the page after that: acres of dusty ground covered in triangular white tents, where some of the wounded were treated.

My grandfather went to see these tents and these wounded men; he must have done; these are his pictures. Then he went back to the seaside again and the girl. Or to another girl like her. What did he think? The pictures don't say. The camera just shut its eye and turned to the next thing. A week later and he was gone himself – into the desert riding a 'lugger' he bought from an Australian; into Palestine, where he fought from 1915 until 1917 and the army sent him to Flanders.

I lost the album a few years back; mislaid it, rather, in one of life's upheavals. But the pictures breathe in my head as if I long ago stepped into them and made them a part of my life. As if I can hear the ships hooting when they come into harbour, and the voices crying as the men are carried ashore, and the silence as my grandfather turns away to walk arm in arm on the sand for a while longer, and puts up his parasol to shade the head of his pretty girl, and together they watch the sun go down.

NICHOLAS HYTNER – Theatre director

I'm afraid I'm going to lower the tone, because I can't get this passage from Marcel Proust's amazing book *In Search of Lost Time* out of my head.

Proust never went to the front. He spent the war working on his phenomenally long novel, and in the last of its seven volumes he gives an account of what life was like in Paris, only an hour away from some of the worst of the bloodshed. The reason I've chosen this passage is that it puts the pity and the terror of the great literature that emerged from the trenches into sharp perspective.

In Proust's Paris, the fashionable parties continue throughout the war. People pretend to care, but in the end what really concerns them is their own pleasure. Monsieur de Charlus barely thinks about how close the Germans are, spending most nights up to no good at all. And who can read about Madame Verdurin's special croissant without a shudder of recognition? A century after the war began, we see new horrors unfold on our television screens almost every day. Our hearts go out to the victims, but how long do we focus on their suffering before we start to think about what we want for breakfast?

FROM *IN SEARCH OF LOST TIME*

So it was that the Verdurins gave dinner-parties (then, after a time, Mme Verdurin gave them alone, for M. Verdurin died) and M. de Charlus went about his pleasures and hardly ever stopped to reflect that the Germans – immobilized, it is true, by a bloody barrier perpetually renewed – were only an hour by car from Paris. The Verdurins, one would imagine, did think about this fact, since they had a political salon in which every evening they and their friends discussed the situation not only of the armies but of the fleets. They thought certainly of those hecatombs of regiments annihilated and passengers swallowed by the waves; but there is a law of inverse proportion which multiplies to such an extent anything that concerns our own welfare and divides by such a formidable figure anything that does not concern it, that the death of unknown millions is felt by us as the most insignificant of sensations, hardly even as disagreeable as a draught. Mme Verdurin, who suffered even more from her headaches now that she could no longer get croissants to dip in her breakfast coffee, had eventually obtained a prescription permitting her to have them specially made in a certain restaurant of which we have spoken. This had been almost as difficult to wrangle with the authorities as the appointment of a general. The first of these special croissants arrived on the morning on which the newspapers reported the sinking of the *Lusitania*. As she dipped it in her coffee and gave a series of little flicks to her newspaper with one hand so as to make it stay open without having to remove her other hand from the cup, 'How horrible!' she said. 'This is something more horrible than the most terrible stage tragedy.' But the death of all these drowned people must have been reduced a thousand million times before it impinged upon her, for even as, with her mouth full, she made these distressful observations, the expression which spread over her face, brought there (one must suppose) by the savour of that so precious remedy against headaches, the croissant, was in fact one of satisfaction and pleasure.

Marcel Proust

MIRANDA HART – Actress, comedian and writer

'Pack Up Your Troubles' is an old music-hall song that became very popular in boosting British morale despite the horrors of the First World War. It was one of a large number of songs aimed at maintaining morale, recruiting for the forces, or defending Britain's war aims.

It is also one of the songs used in the musical *Oh! What a Lovely War*, a satire on the First World War, still performed today.

I love it because it is a song I knew as a child, but I didn't know its resonance until I was much older. It is amazing that a First World War song can be part of a child's culture in the late 1970s and early 1980s. When I sang it, I always found it rousing and inspiring, and so I can only imagine what it did for the troops at the time, in the stark reality of war.

I love it because it could only be British – a stiff upper lip, a great song steeped in great music-hall culture, yet not belittling or undermining the seriousness of the subject. An honourable attempt at lifting spirits. You can smile while singing it. You can cry while singing it. I hope the youth of today are singing it in playgrounds too.

Pack Up Your Troubles in Your Old Kit-Bag

Private Perks is a funny little codger
With a smile – a funny smile.
Five-feet-none, he's an artful little dodger
With a smile – a funny smile.
Flush or broke, he'll have his little joke,
He can't be suppress'd.
All the other fellows have to grin
When he gets this off his chest, Hi!

CHORUS
Pack up your troubles in your old kit-bag,
And smile, smile, smile.
While you've a lucifer to light your fag,
Smile, boys, that's the style.
What's the use of worrying?
It never was worth while, so
Pack up your troubles in your old kit-bag,
And smile, smile, smile.'

Private Perks went a-marching into Flanders
With his smile – his funny smile.
He was lov'd by the privates and commanders
For his smile – his sunny smile.
When a throng of Germans came along
With a mighty swing,
Perks yell'd out, 'This little bunch is mine!
Keep your heads down, boys, and sing, Hi!'

CHORUS

Pack up your troubles in your old kit-bag,
And smile, smile, smile.
While you've a lucifer to light your fag,
Smile, boys, that's the style.
What's the use of worrying?
It never was worth while, so
Pack up your troubles in your old kit-bag,
And smile, smile, smile.'

AFTER

Only Remembered

Fading away like the stars in the morning,
Losing their light in the glorious sun,
Thus would we pass from this earth and its toiling,
Only remembered for what we have done.
Only remembered, only remembered, only remembered
for what we have done,
Thus would we pass from this earth and its toiling,
Only remembered for what we have done.

Only the truth that in life we have spoken,
Only the seed that in life we have sown,
These shall pass onwards when we are forgotten,
Only remembered for what we have done.
Only remembered, only remembered, only remembered
for what we have done,
These shall pass onwards when we are forgotten,
Only remembered for what we have done.

Who'll sing the anthem and who will tell the story?
Will the line hold, will it scatter and run?
Shall we at last be united in glory?
Only remembered for what we have done.
Only remembered, only remembered, only remembered
for what we have done,
Shall we at last be united in glory?
Only remembered for what we have done.

FROM *THE BUTTERFLY LION*

I had seen the wounded men coming from France, blinded, gassed, crippled, and always dreaded seeing Bertie's face amongst them. I had seen the long lists in the newspapers of all the men who had been killed or who were 'missing'. I looked each day for his name and thanked God every time I did not find it. But still he never wrote, and I had to know why. I thought maybe he had been so badly wounded that he could not write, that he was lying in some hospital alone and unloved. So I determined I would become a nurse. I would go to France, and heal and comfort as best I could, and just hope that somehow I might find him. But I soon discovered that amongst so many men in uniform it would be hopeless to go looking for him. I did not even know his regiment, nor his rank. I had no idea where to begin.

I was sent to a hospital some fifty miles behind the lines, not too far from Amiens. The hospital was a converted chateau with turrets and great wide staircases, and chandeliers in the wards. But it was so cold in winter that many of the men died as much from the cold as from their wounds. We did all we could for them, but we were short of doctors and short of medicines. There were always so many men coming in, and their wounds were terrible, so terrible. Each time we saved one it was such a joy to us. In the midst of the suffering all around us, we needed some joy, believe me.

I was at breakfast one morning – it was June of 1918. I was reading a magazine, the *Illustrated London News*, I remember, when I turned the page and saw a face I knew at once. He was older, thinner in the face and unsmiling, but I was sure it was

Bertie. His eyes were deepset and gentle, just as I remembered them. And there was his name: 'Captain Albert Andrews VC'. There was a whole article underneath about what he had done, and how he was still recovering from his wounds in a hospital, a hospital that turned out to be little more than ten miles away. Wild horses would not have kept me from him. The next Sunday I cycled over.

He was sleeping when I saw him first, propped up on his pillows, one hand behind his head. 'Hello,' I said.

He opened his eyes and frowned at me. It was a moment or two before he knew me.

'Been in the wars, have you?' I said.

'Something like that,' he replied.

Michael Morpurgo

MORRIS GLEITZMAN – Author

In Sydney's Botanic Gardens is a bronze memorial.

It shows three horses, kitted out for battle and standing with patient determination on desert sand dunes.

The inscription reads:

ERECTED BY MEMBERS OF
THE DESERT MOUNTED
CORPS AND FRIENDS
TO THE GALLANT HORSES
WHO CARRIED THEM
OVER THE SINAI DESERT
INTO PALESTINE

1915–1918

THEY SUFFERED WOUNDS,
THIRST, HUNGER AND
WEARINESS ALMOST
BEYOND ENDURANCE
BUT NEVER FAILED

THEY DID NOT COME HOME

WE WILL NEVER FORGET THEM.

In fact, one did come home, but only one.

More than 150,000 Australian horses went to the war, often going with their volunteer owners. They were remarkable creatures, the Aussie Walers. Many of the troopers they served so loyally, and whose lives they frequently saved, never stopped mourning their loss.

They were given no medals, our Aussie horses. Just a few words in the gardens.

NICK SHARRATT – Illustrator

I have a sweet tooth and a bit of a fondness for Jelly Babies. But I had no idea about their history until, on a recent visit to the War Poets Collection at Edinburgh Napier University, Craiglockhart Campus, I heard the curator mention how the sweets came into being.

They were introduced in 1918 by the confectionery manufacturer Bassett's to mark the end of the war, and were originally called 'Peace Babies' – little symbols of hope for the next generation after four years of horror. Two decades passed, but production was halted at the outbreak of the Second World War. When the sweets eventually reappeared in the 1950s, they, very sadly, weren't called Peace Babies any more.

JONATHAN STROUD – Author

My chosen piece is a diary entry written by my great-grandfather, George Davison, on Armistice Day, 11 November 1918.

George was born in East Rainton, near Sunderland in the north of England, in 1890. He was by all accounts a kind and gentle man, and I think the photographs of him (many in his army uniform) clearly bear this out. The eldest of nine children, he left school at the age of twelve and found work on the railways. When war was declared, George immediately enlisted. He joined the 3rd Battalion, Durham Light Infantry, and served as a physical training and bayonet instructor before being transferred abroad. He was subsequently wounded, and afterwards transferred to the Army Gymnastic Staff, who were responsible for physical fitness training across the army. George was sent to Mesopotamia, in what is now Iraq, where the British Army was fighting the Turkish Empire. While there, he wrote his diary, and painted watercolour pictures of the people and places he visited.

I love his description of Armistice Day. I think it's beautifully written and very visual. It also conceals much personal grief. Two of George's brothers, Len and Dick, had been killed on the Western Front, Dick just a few weeks before peace was declared. I also like the way that he seeks to justify all the happy roistering. George came from a strict Methodist upbringing, and he was no doubt mindful of what his wife, Elsie, would think when she read about all the drinking!

George went home to his family. His elder daughter, Lenora (named after Len), became my grandmother. He died in 1945.

I was very glad to get back to my billet, for I was anxious to hear from home, and my letters awaited me. Friday, Saturday and Sunday were full of excitement, and all sorts of rumours were being circulated. In the early hours of Monday evening, we were all restless, for we felt we were about to hear good news. About 9.30 our officer came back from 'Advanced Base' telegraph office, and we needed no word from him, for his face betrayed the glorious news. Germany had capitulated. The village was quiet but not for long. We rang fire alarms, bells and gongs, and soon the river front was a scene of joyous activity. Bombs, star shells, and red, white and green maroons lit up the sky, river and trees. Men cheered themselves hoarse, and with tear-filled eyes, they shook hands with all and sundry. Arabs who fled, at the demonstration, came back wonderingly, and were ceremoniously shaken hands with by the delighted soldiers. All decorum for the moment was forgotten, and officers, men, Indians and Arabs, all fraternized in the hour of triumph. People hastily scrambled from their beds to join in the rejoicings, and it was 2 am Tuesday before the final toasts were drank. Everyone in our billet had drink of his own choosing, and we toasted 'The King', 'our soldier lads', 'the silent navy', 'our loved ones at home', 'our Allies', and then we rose, and in silence, drank to 'our dead comrades'. One by one, the men sought their beds, tired but *happy, for we felt we were at the end of all horrors and soon we would again be with our dear ones. Who shall judge a soldier (who has suffered) from going to extremities on such an occasion, for at last we had obtained 'Peace with Victory'.*

Diary Entry by Company Sergeant Major George Davison, Army Gymnastic Staff, Baghdad, 11 November 1918

George Davison

SIR TONY ROBINSON – Actor, comedian and historian

Grandpa Jack

This is a picture of me and my grandpa, Jack Robinson, on our summer holidays in Paignton, on the south-west coast of England. It was taken thirty years after the First World War ended. Grandpa Jack is smiling. He's probably just said something daft. That's how I remember him: joking non-stop, the adults raising their eyebrows because he was such a kid, and me thrilled that a grown-up could say anything so hilarious.

He'd come back from the trenches to his dark little house in 1918. My dad and my Uncle Cyril hardly knew him; they'd been babies when he'd left.

When he walked through the front door, my grandma spread newspapers on the parlour floor. Dad and Uncle Cyril sat huddled on the sofa and watched this strange man take off his private's uniform: first his soldier's tunic, his soldier's boots and his soldier's trousers, then his shirt, his vest and his pants. My grandmother bundled them all up, wrapped them in the paper, and threw them on the fire. Grandpa Jack stood naked in front of the flames watching his clothes burn. Eventually, when all that was left of them was a big, black, smoking lump, he turned his back on them and, without a word, went upstairs and didn't come down till the next morning.

What had his life in the trenches been like? Had he choked on poison gas? Had he lived among rats and pools of blood? Did his comrades die beside him? I don't know. From that day onwards he never spoke to a single person about those four long years. All my memories of Grandpa Jack are of him smiling, like he is in the photograph.

SIR QUENTIN BLAKE – Illustrator

My parents lived in France for ten years after the First World War, before I was born. My father was a surveyor's clerk working for the Imperial War Graves Commission, so that, as I look at recent books about that war, names like Ypres, St Omer, Armentières have some special extra meaning for me. It must have been strange for my young, newly married mother to move immediately to another country amongst acres of regimented white gravestones.

When I was a student, my older brother took me and my parents on an unusual holiday: a tour of British military cemeteries in Northern France, still kept in impeccable order. We made a visit to the *estaminet* that my parents had frequented, kept by a M. and Mme Bouzine. Now, thirty years later, the business was run by the younger generation of the family, but the (now elderly) couple were still there behind the bar. As we came in, Mme Bouzine said: 'Ah, Madame Blake,' and reached down for a bottle of champagne.

My parents must have known them quite well, because we were invited back for a meal. I remember the stewed rabbit being brought to the table in a metal dish, its skull vertical in the middle, its little teeth providing the centrepiece.

My father had served in the war; there too, I think, as a clerk. His friend, who perhaps was his best friend, was called Dicky Herbert; he was in a more dangerous occupation. 'He was in machine guns; he knew he was for it.' I remember towards the end of his life, at a time of quite different bereavement, my father saying – as much to himself as to anyone else – 'Dicky Herbert. He's been dead fifty years.'

SIMON MAYO – Presenter and author

When the history is too enormous, too terrible to comprehend, the small and the trivial can sometimes fill the void. So I have a picture and a song.

My grandmother's photo of her brother, Lieutenant Stanley Gordon Killingback, always sat on her mantelpiece above the radiator, accompanied by her most recent poppy. I'm told I have a slight resemblance to my great-uncle, though if that is true it is lost on me.

In the picture he is in full uniform, neat moustache and a playful smile. His future was bright: he was smart, funny, and a keen amateur actor. His division of the Royal Engineers arrived in France in June 1916; he was killed in action two months later. The official letter to his family announcing his death at the age of twenty-one says he was 'shot through the heart by a German sniper and was killed instantly'. It adds that his final words were, 'Never mind me, you carry on with your duty.'

This is, to put it mildly, unlikely, but its intention to comfort admirable nonetheless. As a child, when the two minutes' silence came, I could never imagine the slaughter of 1914–18, but I could remember my granny's grief, so I thought of that instead.

The song I have chosen is 'No Man's Land' by Eric Bogle. It is sometimes called 'The Green Fields of France', and is a meditation from the grave of a young man called Willie McBride, who also died in 1916. It too tells of a photo *'Forever enshrined behind some glass pane/In an old photograph, torn and tattered and stained'*. My educator here is the peerless June Tabor, who included it on her *Ashes and Diamonds* album in 1977. Its melody is timeless, haunting, instantly memorable and, when combined with the words below, utterly devastating. The lament for Willie becomes a lament for Stanley and the nine million others.

Two deaths among the millions, but a melody for one and a face for the other.

No Man's Land (The Green Fields of France)

Well, how do you do, Private William McBride,
Do you mind if I sit down here by your graveside?
And rest for awhile in the warm summer sun,
I've been walking all day, and I'm nearly done.
And I see by your gravestone you were only 19
When you joined the glorious fallen in 1916,
Well, I hope you died quick and I hope you died clean
Or, Willie McBride, was it slow and obscene?

Chorus:
Did they beat the drum slowly, did they play the pipes lowly?
Did the rifles fir o'er you as they lowered you down?
Did the bugles sound The Last Post in chorus?
Did the pipes play the Flowers of the Forest?

And did you leave a wife or a sweetheart behind
In some loyal heart is your memory enshrined?
And, though you died back in 1916,
To that loyal heart are you always 19?
Or are you a stranger without even a name,
Forever enshrined behind some glass pane,
In an old photograph, torn and tattered and stained,
And fading to yellow in a brown leather frame?

The sun's shining down on these green fields of France;
The warm wind blows gently, and the red poppies dance.
The trenches have vanished long under the plough
No gas and no barbed wire, no guns firing now.

But here in this graveyard that's still No Man's Land
The countless white crosses in mute witness stand
To man's blind indifference to his fellow man.
And a whole generation who were butchered and damned.

And I can't help but wonder, now Willie McBride,
Do all those who lie here know why they died?
Did you really believe them when they told you 'The Cause'?
Did you really believe that this war would end wars?
Well the suffering, the sorrow, the glory, the shame
The killing, the dying, it was all done in vain,
For Willie McBride, it all happened again,
And again, and again, and again, and again.

Eric Bogle

SIR JONATHON PORRITT –
Environmentalist

As an English teacher in London back in the 1970s, it never ceased to amaze me how easily the empathy built between those untested west London kids and the young men in the trenches – there in Flanders simply 'to be killed or kill'. They understood that there would have been no reprieve, even for those who survived their experiences in the trenches, as with Edmund Blunden's 'Can You Remember?'

'CAN YOU REMEMBER?'

Yes, I still remember
    The whole thing in a way;
Edge and exactitude
    Depend on the day.

Of all that prodigious scene
    There seems scanty loss,
Though mists mainly float and screen
    Canal, spire and fosse;

Though commonly I fail to name
That once obvious Hill,
And where we went, and whence we came
To be killed, or kill.

Those mists are spiritual
    And luminous-obscure,
Evolved of countless circumstance
    Of which I am sure;

Of which, at the instance
    Of sound, smell, change and stir,
New-old shapes for ever
    Intensely recur.

And some are sparkling, laughing, singing,
    Young, heroic, mild;
And some incurable, twisted,
    Shrieking, dumb, defiled.

Edmund Blunden

RAYMOND BRIGGS – Illustrator

'Auntie' was the name used by children for any old lady in the nineteen thirties and forties. A child would seldom use the lady's full name – Miss Smith or Mrs Bennett, for example – unless they were an authority figure, such as a school teacher. Nor would a child dream of using the lady's first name, Ethel or Marjorie, but Auntie Ethel and Auntie Marjorie was OK and more polite.

It was odd, because these ladies were not our real aunties, but then, *some* of them were! I was evacuated to a stone cottage in Dorset with Auntie Flo and Auntie Betty. Flo was my real aunt, Betty was not.

As for these ladies being 'old', it was many years before I realized that they were only middle-aged. They belonged to that unlucky generation born around 1900, so they would have been about eighteen in 1918, just the age to be on the look out for a boyfriend and hoping to get married.

To a child, anyone over forty seems 'old', but when you are eighty, as I am now, forty is peanuts!

Boys of my generation, born about 1935, were called up for National Service in the Army or the Air Force aged eighteen. Some were sent out to fight in the Korean War, and many were killed there. Really, they were still schoolboys. Korean War? Ever heard of it?

I was very lucky. I was given 'deferment' from National Service for one year, to complete my four-year art course. I became eighteen in 1952, so finally went into the Army in 1953, the very year the Korean War ended.

Phew! Just missed it. I was lucky with the year I was born; the Aunties were very unlucky with theirs.

AUNTIES

When I was a child,
There were always lots of
Aunties.
They were everywhere.

Some were real aunties –
Mum's umpteen sisters,
Dad's umpteen sisters.
There was no end of them.

Auntie Flo, Auntie Betty,
Auntie Edie, Auntie Marjorie,
Auntie Bertha, Auntie Jessie . . .
The list is endless.

I won't go on,
Except for Auntie Violet,
My favourite auntie,
Killed on a bus in the Blitz.

It seemed quite natural,
Didn't give it a thought.
That was the way the world was –
Lots of old ladies everywhere.

They were called spinsters.
Some were rather quaint.
And looked down upon.
A few were slightly mad.

Then, one day,
When I was grown up,
It dawned on me –

First World War

A million men were missing.
Why hadn't I thought of it before?
The men these women never met,
Never even had the chance to meet.

All dead

These ladies were always kind,
Gentle and loving to me.
Not sour, bitter and resentful,
As they had every right to be.

A million missing men.
A million aunties.

Raymond Briggs

SARAH BROWN – Charity campaigner and writer

Vera Brittain's *Testament of Youth* is the best-known book about the First World War written by a woman. It is one of the most moving and agonizingly painful accounts of personal loss. I remember reading the book as a teenager, and being so gripped by its pages, willing the survival of each young soldier friend sent to the Western Front.

The loss of her fiancé, Roland Leighton; her beloved only brother, Edward Brittain; and numerous close male friends and acquaintances to the horror of trench warfare smashed Vera's safe, predictable world to smithereens. In total, almost nine million soldiers' lives were lost in the Great War, and no one else escaped unhurt or unaffected; all were scarred in some way whether serving in the military or on the Home Front.

Testament of Youth endures for me for two reasons: its powerful story about personal survival beyond desperate grief, and the will to rebuild a life built on strong feminist principles in a fast-changing world.

Women had learned that they could take on the work of men who were at the front, but also discovered that in war's aftermath, this 'lost generation' left huge gaps in their lives – not enough men to marry once the survivors returned, and the women's jobs were not theirs to keep once the war was over. As the world changed for ever, it struggled also to return to normal in a painful way, and Vera Brittain's voice was powerful as she established herself as a wife and mother while campaigning for peace and social change, and the rights of women, in the years that followed.

Testament of Youth, published in 1933, is as much about the role of women, and Vera's own belief that she could have a strong marriage with children, while still maintaining her own career and personal friendships.

Vera Brittain's vivid and intimate writing about the human tragedy of the First World War also acts as a powerful reminder of the importance of bearing witness to historic and troubling times. While the challenges of the twenty-first century are different, they are as complex and challenging. How honestly we tell the story of our time is how we pay it forward to the generations to come.

The passage that stands out in the book for me is where Vera's intended fiancé Roland's clothes are returned to his mother. The visceral recollection of the smell of the clothes evokes so much in one tiny glimpse onto the experience of such deep, personal loss.

FROM *TESTAMENT OF YOUTH*

In Sussex, by the end of January, the season was already on its upward grade, catkins hung bronze from the bare, black branches, and in the damp lanes between Hassocks and Keymer the birds sang loudly. How I hated them as I walked back to the station one late afternoon, when a red sunset turned the puddles on the road into gleaming pools of blood, and a new horror of mud and death darkened my mind with its dreadful obsession. Roland, I reflected bitterly, was now part of the corrupt clay into which the war had transformed the fertile soil of France; he would never again know the smell of a wet evening in the early spring.

🌹 AFTER 🌹

I had arrived at the cottage that morning to find his mother and sister standing in helpless distress in the midst of his returned kit, which was lying, just opened, all over the floor. The garments sent back included the outfit he had been wearing when he was hit. I wondered, and I wonder still, why it was thought necessary to return such relics – the tunic torn back and front by the bullet, a khaki vest dark and stiff with blood, and a pair of blood-stained breeches slit open at the top by someone obviously in a violent hurry. Those gruesome rags made me realise, as I had never realised before, all that France really meant. Eighteen months afterwards the smell of Etaples village, though fainter and more diffused, brought back to me the memory of those poor remnants of patriotism.

'Everything', I wrote later to Edward [Vera's brother, also to die in the war in 1918], 'was damp and worn and simply caked in mud. And I was glad that neither you nor Victor nor anyone who may some day go to the front was there to see. If you had been, you would have been overwhelmed by the horror of war without its glory. For though he had only worn the things when living, the smell of those clothes was the smell of graveyards and the Dead. The mud of France which cover them was not ordinary mud; it had not the usual clean pure smell of earth, but it was as though it was saturated with dead bodies – dead that had been dead a long, long time . . . There was his cap, bent in and shapeless out of recognition – the soft cap he wore rakishly on the back of his head – with the badge thickly coated with mud. He must have fallen on top of it, or perhaps one of the people who fetched him in trampled on it.'

Vera Brittain

MICHAEL LONGLEY – Poet

I wrote 'In Memoriam' in the spring of 1965. It's the first of many elegies for my father, about whom I have been writing obsessively for decades. He enlisted in the London Scottish as a boy-soldier in September 1914, and miraculously survived the Great War. Before he turned twenty-one he was promoted to Captain, and put in charge of soldiers so young his company was nicknamed Longley's Babies. He was seriously wounded at the Battle of High Wood, and was awarded the Military Cross for gallantry. He died in 1960, when I was twenty.

IN MEMORIAM

My father, let no similes eclipse
Where crosses like some forest simplified
Sink roots into my mind; the slow sands
Of your history delay till through your eyes
I read you like a book. Before you died,
Re-enlisting with all the broken soldiers
You bent beneath your rucksack, near collapse,
In anecdote rehearsed and summarised
These words I write in memory. Let yours
And other heartbreaks play into my hands.

Now I see in close-up, in my mind's eye,
The cracked and splintered dead for pity's sake
Each dismal evening predecease the sun,
You, looking death and nightmare in the face
With your kilt, harmonica and gun,
Grow older in a flash, but none the wiser
(Who, following the wrong queue at The Palace,
Have joined the London Scottish by mistake),
Your nineteen years uncertain if and why
Belgium put the kibosh on the Kaiser.

Between the corpses and the soup canteens
You swooned away, watching your future spill.
But, as it was, your proper funeral urn
Had mercifully smashed to smithereens,
The shrapnel shards that sliced your testicles.
That instant I, your most unlikely son,
In No Man's Land was surely left for dead,
Blotted out from your far horizon.
As your voice now is locked inside my head,
I yet was held secure, waiting my turn.

Finally, that lousy war was over.
Stranded in France and in need of proof
You hunted down experimental lovers,
Persuading chorus girl and countesses:
This, father, the last confidence you spoke.
In my twentieth year your old wounds woke
As cancer. Lodging under the same roof
Death was a visitor who hung about,
Strewing the house with pills and bandages,
Till he chose to put your spirit out.

Though they overslept the sequence of events
Which ended with the ambulance outside,
You lingering in the hall, your bowels on fire,
Tears in your eyes, and all your medals spent,
I summon girls who packed at last and went
Underground with you. Their souls again on hire,
Now those lost wives as recreated brides
Take shape before me, materialise.
On the verge of light and happy legend
They lift their skirts like blinds across your eyes.

Michael Longley

'Harmonica' is probably the poem of mine I like best. When I was a boy I brought home from school a mouth organ which my father picked up and started to play quite well. I had never heard him play anything before. In the trenches, during lulls in the fighting, he and his mates had taught themselves to play harmonicas. For years I desperately wanted to write a poem about this, but I had to wait. One day I read how the early Greek philosopher Anaximines believed that air was the basis of creation. He gave me the poem. I wrote 'Harmonica' in November 2001.

HARMONICA

A tommy drops his harmonica in No Man's Land.
My dad like old Anaximines breathes in and out
Through the holes and reeds and finds this melody.

Our souls are air. They hold us together. Listen.
A music-hall favourite lasts until the end of time.
My dad is playing it. His breath contains the world.

The wind is playing an orchestra of harmonicas.

Michael Longley

K. M. PEYTON – Author

My husband is very old and remembers his father as a survivor of the First World War.

He had been injured in the leg and the doctors wanted to amputate it, but he refused to let them. Luckily the leg healed, but he walked with a bad limp. He had brought a souvenir home from the war: it was a German helmet known as a *Pickelhaube*. *Pickel* means 'point' and *Haube* means 'hat', so it was a helmet made of very thick, tough leather with a spike sticking out of the top. What the spike was for was a mystery. Did one run at the enemy head down and stick them in the chest? My husband was very fond of this helmet and loved playing at war, hearing all the stories from his father and his friends. When he was three he was given a set of lead soldiers to play with, and he dug trenches for them in the tiny garden behind his house and set them in. He refused to bring them in at night, as he said all soldiers slept out in the trenches, and his mother was cross because all the paint wore off and they looked old and battered very quickly. But that was how he wanted it.

He didn't know then that when the time came, in the next war, he too would sleep out in the rain like his tin soldiers. He told me once that on a long march they had to sleep when they could go no farther, just where they happened to be, which was in a marsh. He said they sat in their tin hats and lay back against their packs. Perhaps the Pickelhaube would have made a better seat, securely stuck with its spike, and the leather warmer to the bottom.

Later he went to North Africa to fight in the hot desert, but that is another story.

SIR TERRY PRATCHETT – Author

My maternal grandfather never went to war; he was lucky enough to be too young to go to the First World War and too old for the second one, and because he was a rather taciturn individual I never plucked up the courage to ask him if he was happy with that situation, but it was just how the calendar fell. He lived in London when the First World War was gently sliding towards the Second World War.

The war my paternal grandfather fought became known as the Great War, and it was a campaign that simply ate men. It could be called a slaughterhouse. Granddad didn't tell us much, but what was it that he deigned to tell us? Only that it was bad; I think he took the view that I and my cousins were kids, and shouldn't have nightmares. But to me the way he wasn't telling us things said a lot, as if talking about it would call it screaming back.

He was a wonderful gardener and had green fingers, which fortuitously had not been shot off. One day I was chatting to him as he worked in his garden; he broke his silence to tell me about a time when he was a guard at a prisoner-of-war camp near Blandford Forum. One of the prisoners had carved a flute; but my granddad took it away from him. As he told me this, he started to cry with great big sobs. The sobs became a wail that I had never heard from a man before, and it went on and on, which worried me quite a lot – and then suddenly he was all smiles again. And sitting in the garden, we shared his dinner of bread and cheese, with an apple each.

A long time later, as a young journalist, I was talking to a man from the local British Legion, who said, 'We are building a new headquarters and you might be surprised that it will be opened by none other than a local man called Tommy Atkins, who actually fought in that war.' Later, when I got back to the office and told everybody, many of the younger journalists didn't know who Tommy Atkins was; which rather upset me.

In my grandfather's day, the troops were referred to as 'Tommies', a nickname that they had come by in a typically British way. Every young man entering the army had to write his name in his pay book. The powers that were in those days, realizing that some of the young men might have difficulty with reading and writing, had printed the name `Tommy Atkins` to show where they should make their mark. And so, in a very British way, thereafter an enlisted man became known as a 'Tommy'.

In the Second World War my grandfather was, of course, too old to fight on any front other than the Home Front, and joined the Home Guard. Long before *Dad's Army* was on the television he told me a lot about being a gardener by day and waiting for the German invasion by night. It was real *Dad's Army* stuff. Having fought in the Great War, he had a higher rank in the Home Guard than his boss, who was a bigwig in monetary affairs in London, and very snooty, not wanting to take orders from a gardener. On one occasion in a Home Guard parade my granddad's boss got a bit bolshie and decided he wouldn't take an order from his gardener, and got bawled out for it by a full-time ranking officer, who shouted to him, 'Private Kay, you will obey the orders of Corporal Pratchett!'

My grandfather spent a long time in his potting shed after that. But no harm was done, and his boss actually came and apologized. It was definitely a *Dad's Army* moment.

And since it seemed to me that the Tommies were not very well known, much later I wrote a book called *Johnny and the Dead*, where our hero, Johnny Maxwell, meets young Tommy Atkins and learns about that terrible war.

Even now I can remember my granddad, a fairly burly, heavy man, wet with tears . . . Well, it wasn't normal granddad behaviour! But, of course, as I grew older, I knew that those who didn't get killed nevertheless cried.

From *Johnny and the Dead*

'Here, look at this,' said Yo-less.

They clustered around his viewer. He'd found an ancient group photograph of about thirty soldiers, all beaming at the camera.

'Well?' said Wobbler.

'This is from nineteen sixteen,' said Yo-less. 'They're all going off to war.'

'Which one?' said Wobbler.

'The first one, you nerd. World War One.'

'I always wondered why they numbered it,' said Bigmac. 'Like they expected to have a few more. You know. Like Buy Two, Get One Free.'

'Says here,' Yo-less squinted, 'it's the Blackbury Old Pals Battalion. They're just going off to fight. They all joined up at the same time . . .'

Johnny stared. He could hear people's voices, and the background noises of the library. But the picture looked as if it was at the bottom of a dark, square tunnel. And he was falling down it.

Things outside the picture were inky and slow. The picture

was the centre of the world.

Johnny looked at the grinning faces, the terrible haircuts, the jug-handle ears, the thumbs all up.

Even today nearly everyone in the *Blackbury Guardian* had their photo taken with their thumb up, unless they'd won Super Bingo, in which case they were shown doing what the photographer thought was a high kick. The newspaper's one photographer was known as Jeremy the Thumb.

The people in the picture didn't look much older than Bigmac. Well, a couple of them did. There was a sergeant with a moustache like a scrubbing brush, and an officer in jodhpurs, but the rest of them looked like a school photo.

And now he was coming back from wherever he'd been. The picture dropped away again, became just an oblong on a page on a screen. He blinked.

There was a feeling, like—

Like on an aeroplane when it's about to land, and his ears went 'pop'. But it was happening with his brain, instead.

'Anyone know what the Somme is?' said Yo-less.

'No.'

'That's where they went, anyway. Some place in France.'

'Any of them win any medals?' said Johnny, struggling back into the real world. 'That'd be famous. If there's someone in the cemetery with a lot of medals.'

Yo-less spun the wheels of the viewer.

'I'll look ahead a few issues,' he said. 'There's bound to be something if— Hey . . . look at *this* . . .'

They all tried to get under the hood at once. Silence came back as they realized what he'd found.

I knew it was important, Johnny thought. What's happening to me?

'Wow,' said Wobbler. 'I mean – all those names . . . everyone killed in this big battle . . .'

Without saying anything, Johnny ducked into the other reader and wound it backward until he found the cheery photograph.

'Are they listed in alphabetical order?' he said.

'Yes,' said Yo-less.

'I'll read out the names under the photo, then. Um . . . Armitage, K . . . Atkins, T . . .'

'Yes . . . no . . .' said Yo-less. 'Sergeant Atterbury, F . . .'

'Yes.'

'Hey, there's three from Canal Street,' said Wobbler. 'That's where my gran lives!'

'Blazer . . . Constantine . . . Fraser . . . Frobisher . . .'

'Yes . . . yes . . . yes . . . yes . . .'

They carried on to the end of the caption. 'They all died,' said Johnny, eventually.

'Four weeks after the picture was taken. All of them.'

'Except for Atkins, T.,' said Yo-less. 'It says here what a Pals' Battalion was. It says, people all from one town or even one street could all join the Army together if they wanted, and all get sent to . . . the same place.'

'I wonder if they all got there?' said Yo-less. 'Eventually,' he added.

'That's dreadful,' said Bigmac.

'It probably sounded like a good idea at the time. Sort of . . . jolly.'

'Yes, but . . . four weeks . . .' said Bigmac. 'I mean . . .'

'You're always saying you can't wait to join the Army,' said Wobbler. '*You* said you were sorry the Gulf War was over. And all the legs of your bed are off the ground because of all them copies of *Guns and Ammo* underneath it.'

'Well . . . *yeah* . . . war, yeah,' said Bigmac. 'Proper fighting, with M16s and stuff. Not just all going off grinning and getting shot.'

'They all marched off together because they were friends, and got killed,' said Yo-less.

They stared at the little square of light with the names on it, and the long, long line of cheery thumbs.

'Except for Atkins, T.,' said Johnny. 'I wonder what happened to him?'

'It was nineteen sixteen,' said Yo-less. 'If he's still alive, he'll be dead.'

'Any of them on your list?' said Wobbler.

Johnny checked.

'No-oo,' he said, eventually. 'There's one or two people with the same name but the wrong initial. Everyone round here used to get buried up there.'

'Perhaps he came back from the war and moved away somewhere else,' said Yo-less.

'It'd be a bit lonely around here, after all,' said Bigmac.

They looked at him.

'Sorry,' he said.

'I'm fed up with this,' said Wobbler, pushing his chair back. 'It's not real. There's no one special in there. It's just people. And it's creepy. Come on, let's go down to the mall.'

'I've found out what happens to dead bodies when old graveyards are built on,' said Yo-less, as they stepped out into the Tupperware daylight. 'My mum knows. They get taken to some kind of storage place called a necropolis. That's Latin for City of the Dead.'

'Yuk,' said Wobbler.

'Sounds like where Superman lives,' said Bigmac.

'Necropolis!' said Wobbler, zooming his hands through the air. 'By day, mild-mannered corpse – by night . . . duh duh duhduh DAH . . . ZombieMan!'

Johnny remembered the grinning young faces, not much older than Wobbler.

'Wobbler,' he said, 'if you make another joke like that—'

'What?'

'. . . well . . . just don't. Right? I mean it.'

Terry Pratchett

DR ROWAN WILLIAMS –
Bishop, poet and theologian

Like lots of Rudyard Kipling's stories, this one takes a while to understand, but is very vivid and shocking. It's about a nice, comfortable German lady who's in bed with flu and suddenly finds her bedroom visited by the ghosts of five children who've been killed in France or Belgium when their village was attacked, perhaps bombed, by the German army. The lady can't believe that things like this happen in war and tries to pretend that it must all have been an accident . . .

The title and the passage at the end refer to something Jesus says in the Bible about how we try to clean up our souls and pretend everything is all right when it isn't – so that what we're doing is making more room for the devil (the spirit of untruth) to come in.

Kipling wrote this out of his own furious grief and anger at losing his son in the war, and it shows how much he hated the Germans. But the point he makes is not just about Germans – it is about how we so often avoid thinking about what the real cost of war is for innocent people, especially children.

Since the First World War, the methods of war have meant more and more deaths for people not actually involved in fighting. Kipling makes us see that if we pretend this doesn't happen, we're living in an unreal world. Even if you believe (as Kipling did) that war sometimes can't be avoided, it's important to face what it's going to mean for those least able to protect themselves. In other words, Kipling is reminding us that the story of war is not only a story about soldiers.

SWEPT AND GARNISHED

They were there – five of them, two little boys and three girls – headed by the anxious-eyed ten-year-old whom she had seen before. They must have entered by the outer door, which Anna had neglected to shut behind her when she returned with the inhaler. She counted them backward and forward as one counts scales – one, two, three, four, five.

They took no notice of her, but hung about, first on one foot then on the other, like strayed chickens, the smaller ones holding by the larger. They had the air of utterly wearied passengers in a railway waiting-room, and their clothes were disgracefully dirty.

'Go away!' cried Frau Ebermann at last, after she had struggled, it seemed to her, for years to shape the words.

'You called?' said Anna at the living-room door.

'No,' said her mistress. 'Did you shut the flat door when you came in?'

'Assuredly,' said Anna. 'Besides, it is made to catch shut of itself.'

'Then go away,' said she, very little above a whisper. If Anna pretended not to see the children, she would speak to Anna later on.

'And now,' she said, turning toward them as soon as the door closed. The smallest of the crowd smiled at her, and shook his head before he buried it in his sister's skirts.

'Why – don't – you – go – away?' she whispered earnestly.

Again they took no notice, but, guided by the elder girl, set themselves to climb, boots and all, on to the green plush sofa in front of the radiator. The little boys had to be pushed, as they could not compass the stretch unaided. They settled themselves in a row, with small gasps of relief, and pawed the plush approvingly.

'I ask you – I ask you why do you not go away – why do you not go away?' Frau Ebermann found herself repeating the question twenty times. It seemed to her that everything in the world hung on the answer. 'You know you should not come into houses and rooms unless you are invited. Not houses and bedrooms, you know.'

'No,' a solemn little six-year-old repeated, 'not houses nor bedrooms, nor dining-rooms, nor churches, nor all those places. Shouldn't come in. It's rude.'

'"Yes, he said so,' the younger girl put in proudly. 'He said it. He told them only pigs would do that.' The line nodded and dimpled one to another with little explosive giggles, such as children use when they tell deeds of great daring against their elders.

'If you know it is wrong, that makes it much worse,' said Frau Ebermann.

'Oh yes; much worse,' they assented cheerfully, till the smallest boy changed his smile to a baby wail of weariness.

'When will they come for us?' he asked, and the girl at the head of the row hauled him bodily into her square little capable lap.

'He's tired,' she explained. 'He is only four. He only had his first breeches this spring.' They came almost under his armpits, and were held up by broad linen braces, which, his sorrow diverted for the moment, he patted proudly.

'Yes, beautiful, dear,' said both girls.

'Go away!' said Frau Ebermann. 'Go home to your father and mother!'

Their faces grew grave at once.

'H'sh! We *can't*,' whispered the eldest. 'There isn't anything left.'

'All gone,' a boy echoed, and he puffed through pursed lips. 'Like *that*, uncle told me. Both cows too.'

'And my own three ducks,' the boy on the girl's lap said sleepily.

'So, you see, we came here.' The elder girl leaned forward a little, caressing the child she rocked.

'I – I don't understand,' said Frau Ebermann. 'Are you lost, then? You must tell our police.'

'Oh no; we are only waiting.'

'But what are you waiting *for*?'

'We are waiting for our people to come for us. They told us to come here and wait for them. So we are waiting till they come,' the eldest girl replied.

'Yes. We are waiting till our people come for us,' said all the others in chorus.

'But,' said Frau Ebermann very patiently – 'but now tell me, for I tell you that I am not in the least angry, where do you come from? Where do you come from?'

The five gave the names of two villages of which she had read in the papers.

'That is silly,' said Frau Ebermann. 'The people fired on us, and they were punished. Those places are wiped out, stamped flat.'

'Yes, yes, wiped out, stamped flat. That is why and – I have lost the ribbon off my pigtail,' said the younger girl. She looked behind her over the sofa-back.

'It is not here,' said the elder. 'It was lost before. Don't you remember?'

'Now, if you are lost, you must go and tell our police. They will take care of you and give you food,' said Frau Ebermann. 'Anna will show you the way there.'

'No,' – this was the six-year-old with the smile, – 'we must wait here till our people come for us. Mustn't we, sister?'

'Of course. We wait here till our people come for us. All the world knows that,' said the eldest girl.

'Yes.' The boy in her lap had waked again. 'Little children, too – as little as Henri, and *he* doesn't wear trousers yet. As little as all that.'

'I don't understand,' said Frau Ebermann, shivering. In spite of the heat of the room and the damp breath of the steam-inhaler, the aspirin was not doing its duty.

The girl raised her blue eyes and looked at the woman for an instant.

'You see,' she said emphasising her statements with her fingers, '*they* told *us* to wait *here* till *our* people came for us. So we came. We wait till our people come for us.'

'That is silly again,' said Frau Ebermann. 'It is no good for you to wait here. Do you know what this place is? You have been to school? It is Berlin, the capital of Germany.'

'Yes, yes,' they all cried; 'Berlin, capital of Germany. We know that. That is why we came.'

'So, you see, it is no good,' she said triumphantly, 'because your people can never come for you here.'

'They told us to come here and wait till our people came for us.' They delivered this as if it were a lesson in school. Then they sat still, their hands orderly folded on their laps, smiling as sweetly as ever.

'Go away! Go away!' Frau Ebermann shrieked.

'You called?' said Anna, entering.

'No. Go away! Go away!'

'Very good, old cat,' said the maid under her breath. 'Next time you *may* call,' and she returned to her friend in the kitchen.

'I ask you – ask you, *please* to go away,' Frau Ebermann pleaded. 'Go to my Anna through that door, and she will give you cakes and sweeties. It is not kind of you to come in to my room and behave so badly.'

'Where else shall we go now?' the elder girl demanded, turning to her little company. They fell into discussion. One preferred the broad street with trees, another the railway station; but when she suggested an Emperor's palace, they agreed with her.

'We will go then,' she said, and added half apologetically to Frau Ebermann, 'You see, they are so little they like to meet all the others.'

'What others?' said Frau Ebermann.

'The others – hundreds and hundreds and thousands and thousands of the others.'

'That is a lie. There cannot be a hundred even, much less a thousand,' cried Frau Ebermann.

'So?' said the girl politely.

'Yes. *I* tell you; and I have very good information. I know how it happened. You should have been more careful. You should not have run out to see the horses and guns passing. That is how it is done when our troops pass through. My son has written me so.'

They had clambered down from the sofa, and gathered round the bed with eager, interested eyes.

'Horses and guns going by – how fine!' someone whispered.

'Yes, yes; believe me, *that* is how the accidents to the children happen. You must know yourself that it is true. One runs out to look—'

'But I never saw any at all,' a boy cried sorrowfully. 'Only one noise I heard. That was when Aunt Emmeline's house fell down.'

'But listen to me. I am telling you! One runs out to look, because one is little and cannot see well. So one peeps between the man's legs, and then – you know how close those big horses and guns turn the corners – then one's foot slips and one gets run over. That's how it happens. Several times it had happened, but not many times; certainly not a hundred, perhaps not twenty. So, you see, you *must* be all. Tell me now that you are all that there are, and Anna shall give you the cakes.'

'Thousands,' a boy repeated monotonously. 'Then we all come here to wait till our people come for us.'

'But now we will go away from here. The poor lady is tired,' said the elder girl, plucking his sleeve.

'Oh, you hurt, you hurt!' he cried, and burst into tears.

'What is that for?' said Frau Ebermann. 'To cry in a room where a poor lady is sick is very inconsiderate.'

'Oh, but look, lady!' said the elder girl.

Frau Ebermann looked and saw.

'*Au revoir*, lady.' They made their little smiling bows and curtseys undisturbed by her loud cries. '*Au revoir*, lady. We will wait till our people come for us.'

When Anna at last ran in, she found her mistress on her knees, busily cleaning the floor with the lace cover from the radiator, because, she explained, it was all spotted with the blood of five children – she was perfectly certain there could

not be more than five in the whole world – who had gone away for the moment, but were now waiting round the corner, and Anna was to find them and give them cakes to stop the bleeding, while her mistress swept and garnished that Our dear Lord when He came might find everything as it should be.

Rudyard Kipling

ROGER MCGOUGH – Poet

Poems written at the outbreak of the Great War by the likes of Rupert Brooke, Julian Grenfell and Charles Sorley set the moral standard to which eager young volunteers strived to aspire: an overwhelming sense of beauty that comes with the premonition of an early death, and a willingness to give one's life for an idealized England, a country of playing fields and public schools, of decency and cream teas.

By the time Robert Graves had written 'A Child's Nightmare' three years later in 1917, the tone had changed radically. Hundreds of thousands of unwilling conscripts regarded themselves as cannon-fodder being sacrificed in nightmare attacks which had no military justification. Mud, blood and desolation had destroyed those early dreams.

This poem is about a dream, a recurring, horrible one, that a twenty-two-year-old Royal Welch Fusilier wrote in an attempt to give form to the real horror that threatened to engulf him. Despite being wounded, and, in fact, reported dead in 1916, Robert Graves survived the war and enjoyed a long and distinguished life, thus outsmarting the nightmarish Cat with its voice, cruel and flat.

A Child's Nightmare

Through long nursery nights he stood
By my bed unwearying,
Loomed gigantic, formless, queer,
Purring in my haunted ear
That same hideous nightmare thing,
Talking, as he lapped my blood,
In a voice cruel and flat,
Saying for ever, 'Cat! . . . Cat! . . . Cat! . . .'

That one word was all he said,
That one word through all my sleep,
In monotonous mock despair.
Nonsense may be light as air,
But there's Nonsense that can keep
Horror bristling round the head,
When a voice cruel and flat
Says for ever, 'Cat! . . . Cat! . . . Cat! . . .'

He had faded, he was gone
Years ago with Nursery Land,
When he leapt on me again
From the clank of a night train,
Overpowered me foot and hand,
Lapped my blood, while on and on
The old voice cruel and flat
Says for ever, 'Cat! . . . Cat! . . . Cat! . . .'

Morphia drowsed, again I lay
In a crater by High Wood:
He was there with straddling legs,
Staring eyes as big as eggs,
Purring as he lapped my blood,
His black bulk darkening the day,
With a voice cruel and flat,
'Cat! . . . Cat! . . . Cat! . . .' he said,
'Cat! . . . Cat! . . .'

When I'm shot through heart and head,
And there's no choice but to die,
The last word I'll hear, no doubt,
Won't be 'Charge!' or 'Bomb them out!'
Nor the stretcher-bearer's cry,
'Let that body be, he's dead!'
But a voice cruel and flat
Saying for ever, 'Cat! . . . Cat! . . . Cat!'

Robert Graves

ANNE FINE – Writer

Years ago, in a library sale, I came across a quite extraordinary book called *The Winding Road Unfolds*. It was written by Thomas Suthren Hope, who lied to the army about his age and served in the trenches till he was wounded in December 1917. Hope wrote the book in 1936, hoping to warn of the horrors of battle as he, like others, watched the second world war of his lifetime approaching so fast.

The vivid account this man left haunted me. And in *The Book of the Banshee*, my version of a personal record left by the fictional 'William Saffery' equally haunts Will Flowers, who is the very same age and watching the countless grim and explosive scenes in his own family as his tempestuous sister, Estelle, battles through her teenage years.

I wanted to make the book into a comedy – no mean feat for a writer, since the First World War was in no way amusing. But teenage arguments (once they are over) can often seem extremely comical, so I solved the technical problem by following Will's own moods. Young people are mercurial – one minute happy to have a laugh, the next deadly serious. Will finds himself obsessively reading about the soldier William Saffery every night, and can't help but compare Saffery's real wartime battle experiences abroad with those he witnesses at home . . .

From *The Book of the Banshee*

Mum nodded angrily towards the door. 'I'll tell you that young lady's problem. She doesn't know who her friends are. Will is enough of a pain. But Estelle! We do our best, and she just treats us like enemies. At least Will's not like that. At least he's always known who's on his side.'

I couldn't help nodding. But I was not so sure. I don't know who's on whose side. This isn't war. Mind you, sometimes I think it might be a whole lot simpler if we all went round in different coloured uniforms to show where our sympathies lay in each particular battle. 'Oh, look. She's one of us today. She's wearing khaki.' 'Watch out for him. He's just gone up to change back into field grey.'

It probably wouldn't work. Even William Saffery had problems working out who was the enemy. I thought about the time he was scrambling back from a night raid, and a shell fell so close that it blasted him out of his senses. He crawled off, bleeding steadily, the wrong way through No Man's Land, but the sweep of a machine gun over the field of mud and wire soon sent him hurtling into the safety of a shell hole. A flare shot up, and fell in an arc of livid green. In its brief light, he watched bullets flying over the lip of the hole. *Rat-a-tat-tat-tat-tat-tat-tat!* Then suddenly into his private swamp of mud and blood fell someone else in desperate need of shelter. Whoever it was landed heavy as a sandbag. As William rolled to face this new danger, another flare shot up. The bilious light hung for its few long moments in the sky, and William and the other boy looked gravely at one another. Then, with no words, the two of them came to an understanding. Gently, so as not to startle someone no older than himself into a deadly mistake, the boy lifted his arm and pointed out the true direction of William's front line.

In return, William drew back his bayonet.

Will got back safely. That night, he says, he hoped aloud to God the other boy did too. 'I felt no enmity,' he wrote. 'Why should I? Without the dying splutter of the flare, how would I even have known that, where mud and blood had failed to cover it, his uniform was not, like mine, khaki, but the dreaded field grey?'

And that's how I feel about Estelle. Sometimes I even think she has right on her side. Last week, when Gran borrowed me and Estelle to shift some furniture around in her bedroom, we came across an old cardboard box full of photographs at the bottom of the wardrobe. Estelle picked out one of five fancy ladies sitting on a bench at the seaside, dressed up as if they were about to go to church.

In front of them, stabbing the sand with a little wooden spade, was a small child. We couldn't tell if it was a boy or a girl.

'Who's this?' Estelle demanded.

Gran peered at the photo. 'That's my grandmother.'

'Yours?'

Gran gave Estelle a warning look. 'People my age don't come out of tins,' she said tartly.

'And who are all the ladies?'

'My great-grandmother and her four sisters.' She pointed one by one along the line. 'Rose, Elsie, Greta, Matty and Daisy.'

Estelle rooted in the box. A few layers down, she found what was almost the same photo over again. There was the same wide line of white hotels facing the sands, the same tall lampstands curving over the promenade. But this time the child on the beach was old enough to have built a sandcastle with a wide foaming moat and four magnificent turrets.

And this time all the sisters were dressed in black.

'*Everyone* was in mourning by then,' explained Gran. 'It was such a terrible war.' She stroked the photo and a memory came back. 'Do you know, my grandmother once told me that when she ran down to the beach on their first holiday after the war, she couldn't understand why the sea sounded so different. She asked her mother, "Where's that other noise?" and Rose glanced at her sisters. "What other noise, dear?" said Aunty Matty. "The waves sound just the same, surely." But my grandmother persisted. "Yes, the waves sound just the same. But where's the noise you told me was the huge rocks on the sea bed, rolling and banging against one another?" One by one the aunts looked away uneasily and wouldn't answer her. And that was when my grandmother realized for the very first time that, during all those endless summer days spent on the beach, what she'd been hearing was the guns in France.'

I felt quite sick. Gran handed me the photograph to put back in the box, and I couldn't even bear to glance at it again, knowing that, summer after long summer, those aunts had sat in a row and listened to the guns that were killing their husbands and brothers and uncles, and said nothing in front of the children.

'Didn't they *care*?' Estelle demanded.

'Of course they cared,' Gran replied. 'People with self-control don't have any fewer feelings. They felt the same as anyone else when they were handed their black-edged telegrams.'

'But not to say!'

Gran shrugged. 'Stiff upper lip.'

Estelle went mad. 'Fools!' she yelled. 'Idiots! Couldn't they *see* it was a waste? Didn't they *realize* that it was self-control like theirs that let that horrible war go on for years?'

Gran didn't argue with her. Neither did I. Perhaps Estelle's right, and people should speak up more. There is a bit in William Saffery's book when he leans back in a ditch and lets himself daydream about what he would say if he had the chance to show the Big Brass round the battlefield. He'd tell them what he thought of their great 'war to end all wars'. His words burn off the page, and I can hear behind his scorching sarcasms, his bitter wit, the scathing tones of Estelle. Though he probably died of old age before she was born, and she's not read his book, the two of them have a lot in common. Neither would trade a child's unruffled summers on the beach for nothing said about the war in France.

In fact, sometimes at night I get confused. I put down the book and lie in the dark, thinking about what I've read, and when his withering descriptions of all the horrors he sees around him ring in my head, it's Estelle's voice I hear.

That's not surprising. Some of the things they say sound so alike. But he stayed in the war month after month. Oh, he wrote his doubts down secretly when he could; but he kept shooting at those other boys, no older than himself.

Estelle would never have done that. She would have flung her rifle in a ditch rather than be a part of anything about which she had so many doubts.

Who's braver? Who cares more?

Anne Fine

RORY STEWART – Member of Parliament

The title of this poem is taken from the Bible. It describes a world war which will destroy whole nations. Will the writer focus on the battlefield: on guns, so loud that they destroy ears with a single explosion; on the night turned into day by flares and flames; on fear, blood, loyalty, or young men dying?

Thomas Hardy instead chooses to respond to the war with only three images. 'Only a man harrowing clods', 'only thin smoke ... from couch grass', and a girl and boy whispering (he describes them with the medieval words 'maid' and 'wight'). 'Harrowing' is when you drag a sharp object – in this case behind a horse – to break up lumps of earth. It has been done since the beginning of agriculture. The Hebrew word 'sadad' or harrowing appears often in the Old Testament. It happens after the harvest of last year's crop and ploughing, and before the ground is sown with a new crop – usually in late autumn. 'Couch grass' is a weed, found right across the world, which is best torn up by its roots, and burned, in the spring. The man, the old horse, the girl and the boy in the poem have neither features nor names.

All we learn about the exact 'Time' of this Breaking of Nations is a hint of autumn and spring. Hardy does not reveal the dates or places – the centuries or the countries. Farming and whispering are activities which, he reminds us, happened before the war, happened despite the war, and always will. There is no fighting. Why has he chosen to describe war in this way?

In Time of 'The Breaking of Nations'

I

Only a man harrowing clods
　　In a slow silent walk
With an old horse that stumbles and nods
　　Half asleep as they stalk.

II

Only thin smoke without flame
　　From the heaps of couch-grass;
Yet this will go onward the same
　　Though Dynasties pass.

III

Yonder a maid and her wight
　　Come whispering by:
War's annals will cloud into night
　　Ere their story die.

Thomas Hardy

BRIAN PATTEN – Poet

Herbert Read fought in the First World War as an infantry officer. He won the Military Cross in 1917, and membership of the Distinguished Service Order in 1918, and that same year wrote,

> How sick I am of the whole business. Most of the prisoners we took were boys under 20. Our own recent reinforcements were all boys. Apart from uniforms, German and English are as like as two peas, beautiful fresh children, and they are massacred in inconceivable torment.

He returned from that war horrified and disillusioned by the carnage he had witnessed, and became a pacifist. In 1940, during the Second World War, he wrote this poem from the depths of his disillusionment:

> A pacifist is someone who believes in peace, and is against all war.

To a Conscript of 1940

A soldier passed me in the freshly fallen snow,
His footsteps muffled, his face unearthly gray;
And my heart gave a sudden leap
As I gazed on a ghost of five-and-twenty years ago.

I shouted Halt! and my voice had the old accustom'd ring
And he obeyed it as it was obeyed
In the shrouded days when I too was one
Of an army of young men marching

Into the unknown. He turned towards me and I said:
'I am one of those who went before you
Five-and-twenty years ago: one of the many who never returned,
Of the many who returned and yet were dead.

We went where you are going, into the rain and the mud;
We fought as you will fight
With death and darkness and despair;
We gave what you will give – our brains and our blood.

We think we gave in vain. The world was not renewed.
There was hope in the homestead and anger in the streets
But the old world was restored and we returned
To the dreary field and workshop, and the immemorial feud

Of rich and poor. Our victory was our defeat.
Power was retained where power had been misused
And youth was left to sweep away
The ashes that the fires had strewn beneath our feet.

But one thing we learned: there is no glory in the deed
Until the soldier wears a badge of tarnish'd braid;
There are heroes who have heard the rally and have seen
The glitter of a garland round their head.

Theirs is the hollow victory. They are deceived.
But you, my brother and my ghost, if you can go
Knowing that there is no reward, no certain use
In all your sacrifice, then honour is reprieved.

To fight without hope is to fight with grace,
The self reconstructed, the false heart repaired.'
Then I turned with a smile, and he answered my salute
As he stood against the fretted hedge, which was like white lace.

Sir Herbert Read

CHRIS RIDDELL – Illustrator and author

INTRODUCTION TO E.H. SHEPARD'S
"DRAWN FROM MEMORY"

I GREW UP WITH E.H. SHEPARD'S ILLUSTRATIONS. FIRST IN A.A. MILNE'S WINNIE THE POOH BOOKS, THEN KENNETH GRAHAME'S 'WIND IN THE WILLOWS'. LATER, AS A TEENAGER I DISCOVERED SHEPARD'S POLITICAL CARTOONS IN OLD COPIES OF PUNCH AND THEN HIS MASTERLY ILLUSTRATIONS TO SAMUEL PEPYS DIARIES. I ALSO FOUND HIS ILLUSTRATED AUTOBIOGRAPHY, "DRAWN FROM MEMORY". PUBLISHED IN 1957, IT IS A WONDERFULLY EVOCATIVE ACCOUNT OF A LATE VICTORIAN CHILDHOOD IN AN AFFLUENT SUBURB OF NORTH LONDON. ERNEST AND HIS BROTHER CYRIL SHARE ADVENTURES WITH MAIDEN AUNTS, TRADESMEN AND MUCH LOVED SERVANTS IN A TEXT SPRINKLED WITH COMIC AND BEAUTIFULLY OBSERVED ILLUSTRATIONS. AS THE QUOTE ON THE BOOK'S COVER SAYS IT IS "AN ENCHANTED BOOK, WARM WITH MUFFIN FIRES AND BRIGHT WITH UNTRAMMELLED INNOCENCE." EXCEPT, THAT IS, FOR THE DARK SPECTRE OF THE TWENTIETH CENTURY.

THIS APPEARS AT THE END OF CHAPTER SEVEN, "BELOW STAIRS", QUITE UNEXPECTEDLY AND WITH DEVASTATING EFFECT. I WILL NEVER FORGET THE IMPACT IT MADE ON ME AS I READ IT, BRINGING HOME THE CATASTROPHE OF THE FIRST WORLD WAR MORE POWERFULLY THAN ANYTHING ELSE HAD BEFORE. RE-READING IT NOW, THIS PASSAGE STILL BRINGS TEARS TO MY EYES.

CHRIS RIDDELL.

FROM *DRAWN FROM MEMORY*

Martha had very strict ideas of what was right and proper. Honest as the day, she entertained no compromise – things were right or wrong. A Primitive Methodist from the Welsh borders, she loved to talk of the chapel to us children, or to sing us the hymn tunes that she herself had learnt as a child. Sitting by the fire in the nursery, or later in the playroom, she would sing the simple Methodist hymns to us, while Cyril was poring over his beloved stamps and I, perhaps, was drawing in my copy-book. Ethel learnt to play some of these hymns on the piano; she was quick at picking up tunes, and our little piping voices would sing them together.

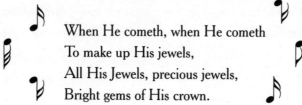

> When He cometh, when He cometh
> To make up His jewels,
> All His Jewels, precious jewels,
> Bright gems of His crown.

Twenty-nine years later I was to hear the words of those hymn tunes again. They were sung by Welsh voices on a dusty shell-torn road in Picardy, as a battalion of Welch Fusiliers marched into battle. I was standing by the roadside, close to what had been Fricourt, when they passed. I was grateful for their song. It seemed as if the men were singing a requiem. For that day I had found my dear brother's grave in Mansell Copse. The spot was marked by simple wooden crosses bearing the names of the Fallen roughly printed on them. It was, and is still, the resting place of over two hundred men of the Devons who fell that Saturday morning in July 1916.

'They will shine like the Morning'

E. H. Shepard

FLORA FERGUSSON – Student

'Gone'

Written by families upon some gravestones in cemeteries near Ypres, where I went three years ago, were touching messages such as 'God gives and He takes away. We will miss Jim'. But the one that struck me hardest was a simple 'Gone'. Aged twelve at the time, I found it difficult to digest this word, engraved into the headstone of a dead man. Why would a family have chosen to write something so cold and stark? In a way, over the past three years I think I have come to understand. After the First World War, hundreds of thousands of bodies were never recovered, so they were literally 'gone'. But in a deeper sense, the war wiped out the hope and joy people had carried with them. That too was gone.

Lots of things have stuck with me from my visit to Ypres – the mournful buglers playing the Last Post at the Menin Gate as the sun set, for example. Writing this during Advent, I particularly remember visiting a desolate field, marked by a simple cross, where the Christmas Truce took place. Apart from a lady who rode by on her horse, we were the only people there. I stood looking down into the valley and wondered what a soldier of 1914 would have thought, standing in the same place . . . and I began to picture what happened.

On 24 December soldiers from both sides ceased fighting, came together and played a game of football. The next day they were killing each other.

Turn to pages 123 and 129 to read more about the Christmas Truce.

One man might have found himself killing another whose hand he had shaken the day before. My perhaps childish mind prompted me to ask, 'Why didn't the soldiers simply say to their officers, "Sorry, we have made friends and just won't fight, even if you threaten to shoot us"?'

Winston Churchill wrote something similar in a letter home to his wife:

What would happen, I wonder, if the armies suddenly and simultaneously went on strike and said some other method must be found of settling this dispute?

Leaders chivvying on the war could not afford to shoot all their men so, with hope, if they had all protested together then they would have survived. Or the winners of the war could have been decided by a football match.

My whirring mind stopped when I wondered what would have happened, after the Christmas Truce, if there had been women fighting instead of men. As my mind stopped, the war seemed to also. After making friends during a truce, a woman could never have continued to fight the next day. Why? On the whole, women are more prone to emotion than men, and are perhaps less proud and stubborn. So maybe war would have ended there for a woman.

For many soldiers fighting in the First World War, it made no difference which country won or lost. They died anyway. But what happened during the Christmas Truce made a difference. The bond between soldiers who had no idea how to communicate in each other's language yet could still shake hands and smile – this would be remembered. This would still matter after they were 'gone'.

MAGGIE FERGUSSON – Biographer and writer

In this centenary year, we'll all be reflecting on the horrors of the First World War; the tragedy of lives cut short and the heroism of those who died – and rightly so. But we should remember too the soldiers who did not die, who carried home from the Flanders mud memories of carnage and misery, and then had to try to make sense of the future.

Like so many who went off to fight, my grandfather had grown up in what now seems a kind of rural idyll. He spent his boyhood in Claughton, a tiny Lancashire village between the Calder and the Brock valleys, the youngest of eight children – four boys, four girls. An album of old photographs evokes an apparently endless, carefree Edwardian summer. Men with turned-up trousers and rolled-up shirtsleeves carry cricket bats and tennis rackets. Women in ankle-length skirts and pin-tucked blouses laugh from the shade of parasols. A farmer cuts a field of hay with a horse-drawn scythe.

Then we reach the summer of 1918. My grandfather, now nineteen, stands outside the family home, a young soldier, about to be commissioned into the Coldstream Guards. He looks straight at the camera, eager and smiling.

So the next photograph comes as a shock. He is back in England, lying in an iron-framed bed, wounded. Again, he looks straight at the camera, but now his expression is far away, haunted and desperately sad.

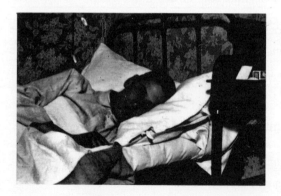

A part of the story that unfolded between these two photographs is told in the diary my grandfather kept when he went to war. On Tuesday 16 July 1918 he sails across the English Channel and his mood is high-spirited, almost romantic:

Southampton Water was wonderful. The sunset was straight up the 'water' and the light made the sea quite green and gold and the horizon was all misty with sunlight.

He reads *The Jungle Book* to send him to sleep.

For a time, his new life in France does not at all conform to the image most of us have of the First World War. Instead of mud and trenches, he describes games of polo, champagne and excellent food – including chickens sent out to him from Claughton. Time hangs heavy. He longs to go 'up the line' – 'anything is better than waiting'. On a hot afternoon in August, he dreams of home:

Far above me six curlew are slowly winging seawards. I can hear them calling to each other. I can see them now with their long beaks. The whole air is too full of perfect pure happiness to last . . . I wonder if anyone ever loved a place as I love Claughton.

Then, as he moves closer to the front, things take a grimmer turn. He is gassed. He finds body parts by the sides of the road. He watches a German soldier dying in a prisoner-of-war 'cage':

His face was haggard and grey with deep lines in it. His throat was all bound up and he looked ghastly . . . I saw one of the intelligence officers give [him] a cup of something. His smile of gratitude was simply childlike.

A number of his own friends also die.

22 August: Today we buried Rupert and Roderick. As each body was swung off the stretcher the head fell back and the form disappeared from view. As Rupert's body was swung off the stretcher, I saw that the back of his blanket was all wet. A shell took most of his back away. This gave his form a curious flat look.

30 August: Gerard Brassey died of wounds. Poor boy . . . It seems so odd to think that someone one has known only as a boy, very young at that, and very fond of enjoying himself, should now have actually experienced the beyond . . . Maxwell-Stuart has died of wounds. He is the fourth boy of that family to go.

The last diary entry is written on Saturday 14 September. My grandfather feels 'bored' and 'restless'. 'Something is going to happen,' he writes. 'Tomorrow we go up the line.' He feels 'mortally afraid'. Shortly afterwards, leading his men 'over the top', and turning to urge them all to keep their heads down, he was hit by a hand grenade. A jagged lump of metal penetrated his cheekbone just below his left eye, passed through the narrow space between the bottom of his brain and the roof of his mouth, and broke his right jaw. He would later describe with affection and gratitude the gentle kindness of the German prisoner of war who carried him to safety on a stretcher – 'fatherly' was the word he used of him. He was not expected to live.

What my grandfather's diary never mentions is that three years earlier, in 1915, his eldest brother, Tom, had died, aged twenty-seven, of wounds received at the battle of Neuve Chapelle. The following year, his uncle Henry died in Devil's Wood on the Somme. So by the time my grandfather was wounded, his mother had already lost a son and a brother – not to mention four of her five nephews: Theodore, killed at Illies in October 1914, aged twenty-six; John, killed at Pilkin, Flanders, in April 1915, aged twenty-five; Hugh, killed on the Somme in July 1916, aged nineteen; and Francis, killed on the Vimy Ridge in April 1917, aged twenty-one. My great-grandmother was a brilliant, gifted woman, with a depressive streak. When the news reached Claughton that my grandfather had been wounded, probably fatally, she took her own life.

In almost every village in England, the names of those who died for their country in the Great War are engraved on plinths and obelisks and memorial stones. But who knows how many died of grief?

There was more tragedy to come. In the summer of 1919, another of my grandfather's brothers, Roger, serving with the Expeditionary Force in Russia, was blown up defusing a mine that was floating towards a hospital barge on the River Dvina.

The doctors never managed to remove the metal from my grandfather's head. It lodged there for the next seventy-odd years, along with a deep crevice where it had entered his face. From time to time he was afflicted with moods of great darkness, when the world seemed bleak. He was easily moved to tears – 'the gift of tears', he called it. The wound and the tears gave him an air of dignity and quiet authority.

He was a man of deep faith. 'I suppose,' he wrote, looking back over his war diaries in old age, wondering why he had been spared, 'there was something the good Lord wanted me to do with my life.' He had a long and happy marriage, was father to seven children, and was successful in his career. Yet, despite the demands of family and work, he devoted himself unceasingly to helping others – 'always', as the priest said at his requiem mass, 'wanting to help them forwards to fuller life and growth.' He supported orphaned and abandoned children, young offenders from deprived homes, and disabled ex-servicemen. In the summer, he accompanied sick and handicapped people on pilgrimages to Lourdes. 'He was,' as a friend wrote after his death, 'one of the goodest men I've ever known.'

'True heroism,' the poet George Mackay Brown believed, 'is to try to live this one day well, whatever the circumstances.' If that is so, then my grandfather was as much a hero as his brothers who died in the war.

CAROL HUGHES – Nurse, and wife of the late Ted Hughes

In this poem, Ted describes his father's near-death experiences during the First World War, his post-war decoration for heroism at Ypres, the DCM – and the nightmares he endured for many years beyond the war's end.

Ted wrote the poem after William Hughes's death in 1981. It evokes his spirit with deep humility and filial love, yet the writer yearns to comprehend his own inability to question the father during his lifetime about the horrors and hopelessness of warfare suffered by him and countless others.

FOR THE DURATION

I felt a strange fear when the war-talk,
Like a creeping barrage, approached you.
Jig and jag I'd fitted much of it together.
Our treasure, your D.C.M. – again and again
Carrying the wounded
Collapsing with exhaustion. And as you collapsed
A shell-burst
Just in front of you lifting you upright
For the last somnambulist yards
Before you fell under your load into the trench.
The shell, some other time, that buried itself

Between your feet as you walked
And thoughtfully failed to go off.
The shrapnel hole, over your heart – how it spun you.
The blue scar of the bullet at your ankle
From a traversing machine-gun that tripped you
As you cleared the parapet. Meanwhile
The horrors were doled out, everybody
Had his appalling tale.
But what alarmed me most
Was your silence. Your refusal to tell.
I had to hear from others
What you survived and what you did.

Maybe you didn't want to frighten me.
Now it's too late.
Now I'd ask you shamelessly.
But then I felt ashamed.
What was my shame? Why couldn't I have borne
To hear you telling what you underwent?
Why was your war so much more unbearable
Than anybody else's? As if nobody else
Knew how to remember. After some uncle's
Virtuoso tale of survival
That made me marvel and laugh –
I looked at your face, your cigarette
Like a dial-finger. And my mind
Stopped with numbness.

Your day-silence was the coma
Out of which your night-dreams rose shouting.
I could hear you from my bedroom –

The whole hopelessness still going on,
No man's land still crying and burning
Inside our house, and you climbing again
Out of the trench, and wading back to the glare

As if you might still not manage to reach us
And carry us to safety.

Ted Hughes

Observed by his two sons William Hughes, a survivor of Gallipoli (1915), walks gingerly across a frosty courtyard. He is elderly now, frail-boned and cautious in his footwork. The sons laugh a little, not knowing why, but perhaps nervously in that embarrassed way we all do sometimes.

With hindsight, the writer reflects on this in the poem, and on the engines of war, the brave hopes and patriotism of those sucked in – and ultimately the senselessness of it all. War – that consumes the life-force even of those who survive.

THE LAST OF THE 1ST/5TH LANCASHIRE FUSILIERS

A Souvenir of the Gallipoli Landings

The father capers across the yard cobbles
Look, like a bird, a water-bird, an ibis going over pebbles
We laughed like warships fluttering bunting.

Heavy-duty design, deep-seated in ocean-water
The warships flutter bunting.

A fiesta day for the warships
Where war is only an idea, as drowning is only an idea
In the folding of a wave, in the mourning
Funeral procession, the broadening wake
That follows a ship under power.

War is an idea in the muzzled calibre of the big guns.
In the grey, wolvish outline.
War is a kind of careless health, like the heartbeat
In the easy bodies of sailors, feeling the big engines
Idling between emergencies.

It is what has left the father
Who has become a bird.
Once he held war in his strong pint mugful of tea
And drank at it, heavily sugared.
It was all for him
Under the parapet, under the periscope, the look-out
Under Achi Baba and the fifty billion flies.

Now he has become a long-billed, spider-kneed bird
Bow-backed, finding his footing, over the frosty cobbles
A wader, picking curiosities from the shallows.

His sons don't know why they laughed, watching him
    through the window
Remembering it, remembering their laughter
They only want to weep

As after the huge wars
Senseless huge wars
Huge senseless weeping.

CATHERINE JOHNSON – Writer and screenwriter

We have no claim to the stars
Nid oes gennym hawl ar y sêr

Hedd Wyn (Blessed Peace) was the pen name of Ellis Humphrey Evans, a shepherd and poet from North Wales who died at the Battle of Passchendaele on 31 July 1917, aged thirty. Only a few weeks later his final poem, 'Yr Arwr' (The Hero), was awarded the highest accolade in Welsh literature, the Bardic Chair at the National Eisteddfod, the Welsh language festival of poetry and arts which is held every year.

Hedd Wyn had won many prizes for his poetry before the war, and as farming was a protected profession he stayed at home until the spring of 1917, when his family were called to send one of their sons to fight. Hedd Wyn joined up to protect his younger brother, Robert. He spent only four short months as a soldier and died on the Pilckem Ridge when a nose-cap shell hit him in the stomach and he was mortally wounded; 31,000 other Allied soldiers died on that day.

When the prize is announced at the National Eisteddfod, the name of the winning poet is called three times. That year, 1917, it was held in the first week of September, in the presence of then Prime Minister, David Lloyd George. But when the winner was read out, there was no answer; the hall fell silent. In honour of

Hedd Wyn, the Chair was draped in black cloth and the ceremony continued around the empty seat, a festival of tears.

His poetry is as moving and affecting as any of the English war poets and he is well known in Wales, but as he wrote in his mother tongue and there are only a few translations, his work isn't as well known as Owen's or Sassoon's. His war poetry includes 'Rhyfel, Yr Arwr Nid a'n Dango', and 'Y Blotyn Du'.

Y Blotyn Du

Nid oes gennym hawl ar y sêr,
Na'r lleuad hiraethus chwaith,
Na'r cwmwl o aur a ymylch
Yng nghanol y glesni maith.

Nid oes gennym hawl ar ddim byd
Ond ar yr hen ddaear wyw;
A honno syn anhrefn i gyd
Yng nghanol gogoniant Duw.

The Black Spot

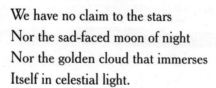

We have no claim to the stars
Nor the sad-faced moon of night
Nor the golden cloud that immerses
Itself in celestial light.

We only have a right to exist
On earth in its vast devastation,
And it's only man's strife that destroys
The glory of God's creation.

Hedd Wyn
(translation by Alan Lwyd)

FRANK GARDNER – Journalist

For me, there will always be something inexplicably sad and nostalgic about Vaughan Williams's piece of music, *The Lark Ascending*.

He composed it in 1914, just as Europe was teetering on the edge of the abyss of the First World War. Yet this music could not be further from the sinister rumble of imminent battle that appears in Gustav Holst's equally memorable *Mars, God of War*, in *The Planets* suite. Instead it evokes a tranquil time when Britain was riding high, having mastered the secrets of the Industrial Revolution, and memories of Queen Victoria's sixty-four-year reign were still fresh. Yet whole countries were now sleepwalking into a conflict that would wipe out a generation.

As that war broke out, Vaughan Williams was on holiday in Margate, and Royal Navy ships were gathering offshore. It is said that somebody spotted him scribbling notes for a composition and mistook him for a German spy writing secret messages, so that a policeman promptly arrested him. He was later released.

I was still a child when my mother stopped what she was doing in the kitchen, turned up the radio and said, 'Listen to this!' as *The Lark Ascending* began. Naturally I was busy imagining a skylark singing as it rose up into the sky, an image so exquisitely conjured up by the notes of a violin. But she told me then it spoke of an innocent era when everyone was unaware of the horrors that were to come. Of course, there were plenty of other troubles in our society at the time, but all were eclipsed by the Great War.

Years later I was in Ypres, in Belgium, with my girlfriend at the time, visiting one of the great battlefields of the First World War where 300,000 British and Commonwealth troops died. A group of aged veteran soldiers stood or sat in wheelchairs, looking down, lost in thought, on one of the original trenches that had been preserved. A Scots piper played a lament on the bagpipes and a breeze whispered softly through the trees. When the piper finished, there was absolute silence, save for the song of a lark, ascending into that blue Belgian sky, soaring above the ground where so many had perished, so many years ago.

THE FIRST WORLD WAR –
A TIMELINE OF KEY EVENTS

DATE	EVENT
28/06/1914	Archduke Franz Ferdinand is assassinated in Sarajevo, Bosnia.
28/07/1914	Austria-Hungary declares war on Serbia.
03/08/1914	Germany declares war on France and Belgium.
04/08/1914	Britain declares war on Germany.
12/08/1914	Britain declares war on Austria-Hungary.
22/11/1914	Trenches are established along the entire Western Front.
19/01/1915	Germany's first Zeppelin attack on British soil takes place, killing five civilians.
22/04/1915	Second Battle of Ypes begins with the first use of poison gas by Germany.
25/04/1915	Battle of Gallipoli begins.
23/05/1915	Italy declares war on Austria-Hungary.
25/05/1915	Prime Minister Asquith creates a new coalition government.
31/05/1915	The first Zeppelin raid on London kills seven and injures 35.
25/09/1915	At the Battle of Loos, the British use poison gas for the first time.
07/12/1915	British evacuation from Gallipoli begins.
27/01/1916	Conscription introduced in Britain.
01/07/1916	The first day of the Battle of the Somme; over 19,000 British soldiers are killed.
02/09/1916	The first Zeppelin is shot down over Britain.
18/11/1916	Battle of the Somme ends without a clear victor.
15/03/1917	Tsar Nicholas II abdicates.
06/04/1917	US declares war on Germany.
13/06/1917	Germans launch the first major aircraft raid over London; 162 people are killed and 432 injured.
12/10/1917	The British launch their latest assaults at Ypres against the Passchendaele Ridge.
19/10/1917	The last airship raid on Britain is carried out by 11 Zeppelins.

26/10/1917	The Second Battle of Passchendaele begins with 20,000 men of the Third and Fourth Canadian Divisions advancing up the hills of the salient. It cost the Allies 12,000 casualties for a gain of a few hundred yards.
21/03/1918	Second Battle of the Somme, marked by the German Spring Offensive, the 'Kaiserschlacht'. Germans attack along a 50-mile front south of Arras.
05/04/1918	Germany calls off Operation Michael, ending the Second Battle of the Somme.
19/05/1918	33 German aircraft launch a final raid on London. 49 civilians are killed and 177 wounded.
10/10/1918	Allied victory at the Battle of Saint-Quentin Canal pierces the Hindenburg Line.
03/10/1918	Germany asks the Allies for an armistice.
08/11/1918	Armistice negotiations between the Allies and Germany begin in Ferdinand Foch's railway carriage HQ at Compiègne.
09/11/1918	Kaiser Wilhelm II abdicates and flees to Holland.
11/11/1918	Armistice Day. The Armistice is signed at 5.00 a.m. and comes into effect at 11.00 a.m. Canadian Private George Lawrence Price is the last soldier to die in action on the Western Front, at 10.57 a.m.
29/06/1919	Treaty of Versailles signed.

USEFUL WEBSITES

BBC WWI Centenary website:
http://www.bbc.co.uk/remembrance/

A Multimedia History of WWI:
http://www.firstworldwar.com/

The British Library:
http://www.bl.uk/world-war-one

THE FIGHTING
Battlefields on the Western Front: **http://www.greatwar.co.uk/**
The German U-boats of both World Wars: **http://www.uboat.net/**
Aviation: **http://www.wwiaviation.com**

THE PEOPLE
The British Army in WW1: **http://www.1914-1918.net/**
Articles about those who served during the world wars:
http://blog.guidedbattlefieldtours.co.uk/
Australian and New Zealand Army Corps: **http://www.anzacs.net/**
The Christmas Truce: **http://www.christmastruce.co.uk/**

POETRY
The War Poets Association: **http://www.warpoets.org/**

PHOTOGRAPHY
The WWI Document Archive:
http://www.gwpda.org/photos/greatwar.htm

ART
Sandham Memorial Chapel:
http://www.nationaltrust.org.uk/sandham-memorial-chapel/

AFTER
After the War: **www.aftermathww1.com**

Contributors

HRH The Duchess of Cornwall is married to HRH The Prince of Wales. Her Royal Highness supports many charities as Patron or President, and has a particular focus on those which promote reading and writing.

Jenny Agutter is an actress who came to the British public's attention in The Railway Children. She has worked in film, television and theatre (winning an Emmy for her role in The Snow Goose and a BAFTA for Equus). She plays Sister Julienne in the BBC1 drama Call the Midwife. In 2012 she received an OBE for her services to charity.

David Almond is an award-winning children's author. His first novel, Skellig, won the Whitbread Children's Book Award and the Carnegie Medal. His other books have received the Nestlé Smarties Book Prize (Gold and Silver Awards), the Whitbread Children's Book Award, and have twice been shortlisted for the Carnegie Medal.

Lord Paddy Ashdown is a politician and diplomat who served as Member of Parliament for Yeovil (1983–2001), leader of the Liberal Democrats (1988–99) and the International Community's High Representative for Bosnia and Herzegovina (2002–6). He is Chair of the Liberal Democrats 2015 General Election Team and has written several books on his life in politics and political history; the most recent, The Cruel Victory, was published in June 2014.

Sir Roger Bannister is a former athlete, doctor and academic. He was the first man to run a mile in under four minutes before becoming a distinguished neurologist and Master of Pembroke College, Oxford. He was knighted for his services to sport in 1975.

Ben Barnes is an actor who has starred in films including The Chronicles of Narnia and Dorian Gray. He starred as Stephen Wraysford in Sir Trevor Nunn's 2010 stage adaptation of Sebastian Faulks' novel *Birdsong*.

Julian Barnes is the author of eleven novels, including *The Sense of an Ending*, which won the Man Booker Prize in 2011. His work has been translated into over forty languages.

Antony Beevor is a historian and author of several books, including *Stalingrad* (winner of the Samuel Johnson Prize, the Wolfson Prize for History and the Hawthornden Prize for Literature) and *Berlin – The Downfall 1945* (winner of the Longman-History Today Trustees Award).

Malorie Blackman is an acclaimed children's author who has written over sixty books and is acknowledged as one of today's most imaginative and creative writers for young readers. In 2008 she was appointed an OBE for her contribution to children's literature and is the Children's Laureate 2013–15.

Sir Quentin Blake is a an artist, illustrator and children's writer. As well as creating his own picture books, he has collaborated with writers such as Roald Dahl, Michael Rosen, John Yeoman, Russell Hoban and Michael Morpurgo. He has won many prizes, including the Hans Christian Andersen Award for Illustration, the Eleanor Farjeon Award and the Kate Greenaway Medal, and in 1999 he was appointed the first Children's Laureate. In 2013 Blake was knighted for his services to illustration.

John Boyne is the author of eight novels for adults and four for younger readers, including the international bestseller *The Boy in the Striped Pyjamas*, which was made into a Miramax feature film.

Theresa Breslin is the author of over thirty books for children and young adults, and her work has been adapted for radio, stage and television. *Divided City* was shortlisted for ten book awards and won two, and was chosen for the One Book cross-border reading project in Ireland set up by the EU Programme for Peace and Reconciliation. She was awarded the Carnegie Medal for her book *Whispers in the Graveyard*.

Raymond Briggs is a children's author and illustrator. Several of his books have been made into highly acclaimed animated films, including *The Snowman* and *When the Wind Blows*. Briggs has twice been awarded the Kate Greenaway Medal – for The Mother Goose Treasury and Father Christmas.

Sarah Brown is President of the charity PiggyBankKids and Patron of a number of charities, including Wellbeing of Women, Women's Aid and Maggie's Cancer Caring Centres. She is married to former Prime Minister Gordon Brown, and in 2011 published *Behind the Black Door*, a memoir about her time in Downing Street.

Shami Chakrabarti is Director of the human rights organization Liberty. She is Chancellor of Oxford Brookes University, a Visiting Fellow of Nuffield College, Oxford, and a Master of the Bench of Middle Temple. Her first book, *On Liberty*, is published this year.

Emma Chichester Clark is a children's book illustrator and author, best known for her picture book series *Blue Kangaroo*. Clark studied illustration under Quentin Blake and in 1988 won the Mother Goose Award for best newcomer.

Eoin Colfer is an author of books for children and young adults. He began writing plays at an early age and, as an adult, continued to write. He is best known for his popular series of children's books, *Artemis Fowl*.

Jilly Cooper is a journalist, author and media superstar. The author of many number one bestselling books, she was appointed an OBE for services to literature in 2004.

Susan Cooper is a world-renowned author of children's books. Her classic *The Dark* Is Rising sequence has won the Newbery Medal and was twice shortlisted for the Carnegie Medal. Her *Boggart* titles have won the Scottish Arts Council Children's Book Award. As well as writing novels, Susan Cooper has written for the theatre and for television.

Richard Curtis is an award-winning film director and script writer, and the creator of *Four Weddings and a Funeral, Love Actually, Notting Hill* and *Mr Bean*. Along with Rowan Atkinson and Ben Elton, he co-wrote the much-loved sitcom *Blackadder*.

Laura Dockrill is an author, performance poet, illustrator and short story writer. She was named one of the top ten literary talents by *The Times*, and one of the top twenty 'hot faces to watch' by *ELLE* magazine. Her first book for children, *Darcy Burdock*, was shortlisted for the Waterstones Children's Book Prize.

Ben Elton is an award-winning playwright, librettist, director, comedian and the author of fourteen internationally bestselling novels. His television writing credits include *The Young Ones, Blackadder* and *The Thin Blue Line*.

Lissa Evans became a radio and television producer – her credits include *Room 101, Father Ted* and *The Kumars at Number 42* – following a brief career in medicine. She has written books for both adults and children, including *Small Change for Stuart*, which was shortlisted for the 2011 Costa Children's Book Award.

Maggie Fergusson is Director of the Royal Society of Literature and Literary Editor of *The Economist*'s bi-monthly magazine, *Intelligent Life*. She is the award-winning author of biographies of George Mackay Brown and Michael Morpurgo. Her elder daughter, **Flora**, is studying for her GCSEs at Sacred Heart High School in Hammersmith.

Frank Field is a Labour Party politician who has been the MP for Birkenhead since 1979. He served as the Minister of Welfare Reform (1997–8). He is author of many books on social policy, including *Saints and Heroes: Inspiring Politics* (2010).

Anne Fine is the author of over fifty highly acclaimed books for children. She has won numerous awards, including the Guardian Children's Fiction Prize, and both the Whitbread Children's Book of the Year and the Carnegie Medal twice over. Anne was appointed Children's Laureate (2001–3), and in 2003 she became a Fellow of the Royal Society of Literature and was awarded an OBE.

Klaus Flugge is a children's publisher. In 1976 he set up his own publishing company, Andersen Press, and has since published over 2,000 books for children. In 1999, Flugge received the Eleanor Farjeon Award for his outstanding contribution to children's books, and in 2010 became only the second publisher to be awarded honorary membership of the Youth Libraries Group.

Michael Foreman is an acclaimed children's author and illustrator. Amongst Michael's most personal creations is his award-winning trilogy of books, *War Boy*, *War Game* and *After the War Was Over*. They draw on Michael's own experience of the Second World War and its aftermath, and his family's experience of the First World War.

Mariella Frostrup is a journalist, broadcaster and campaigner. She presents *Open Book* on BBC Radio 4 and has a regular column in the *Observer*. Frostrup is a respected arts critic and BAFTA member who has sat on the judging panel of a number of the UK's top arts prizes, including the Man Booker Prize, the Evening Standard Film Awards, the Turner Prize, the Stirling Prize and the Costa Book of the Year.

Frank Gardner is the BBC's Security Correspondent, reporting for television and radio on issues of domestic and international security, notably on Al-Qaeda-related terrorism. He has written for *The Economist*, the *Sunday Times*, the *Daily Telegraph* and *Time Out*, and has been published in *The Best of Sunday Times Travel Writing*. In 2005 he was appointed an OBE for services to journalism.

Jamila Gavin has written numerous critically acclaimed novels and collections of short stories. Her book *Coram Boy* won the Whitbread Children's Book Award in 2000, and was shortlisted for the Carnegie Medal before being adapted for the stage.

Morris Gleitzman is a bestselling children's author. His books explore serious and sometimes confronting subjects in humorous and unexpected ways. His titles include *Two Weeks with the Queen, Grace, Doubting Thomas, Bumface, Give Peas a Chance, Pizza Cake, Too Small to Fail, Once, Then, Now and After*. His books are published in more than twenty countries.

Dame Evelyn Glennie is an award-winning percussionist and composer, and is considered the first person in musical history to successfully create a full-time career as a solo percussionist. Glennie was appointed an OBE for services to music in 1993 and was promoted to Dame Commander of the British Empire in 2007.

Howard Goodall is an award-winning composer of choral music, stage musicals, film and TV scores, and a distinguished broadcaster. He was appointed a CBE in the 2011 New Year Honours for services to music education.

Miranda Hart is a comedy writer, comedian and actress. Hart writes and stars in the hit BBC comedy *Miranda* and stars as Camilla 'Chummy' Cholomondely-Browne in the BBC drama *Call the Midwife*. Hart's first book, *Is It Just Me?*, was published in 2013.

Anne Harvey is an actress, broadcaster and a poetry and literary anthologist. She has edited numerous poetry anthologies and in her work as an actress has portrayed many literary heroes, including the author Eleanor Farjeon whose life, along with that of the poet Edward Thomas, she has researched and written about extensively.

Charlie Higson is an author and TV writer and producer. Higson has written a number of novels for adults and children, including the bestselling *Young Bond* and *The Enemy series*, and his television credits include the hit comedy series *The Fast Show*.

Anthony Horowitz is an award-winning writer and screenwriter. He is the author of the internationally successful *Alex Rider* series, which was adapted into a film for which he wrote the screenplay. Horowitz's television credits include *Midsomer Murders* and *Foyle's War*. In 2014 he was awarded an OBE for services to literature.

Carol Hughes was married to the late poet and children's author Ted Hughes (Poet Laureate 1984–98) from 1970 until his death in 1998. In 2006 she opened the Hughes Poetry Trail at Stover Country Park in Devon.

Shirley Hughes is a children's author and illustrator. As well as illustrating the work of prominent children's authors, notably Dorothy Edwards's *My Naughty Little Sister* series, she has written and illustrated over fifty books, including *Dogger* and the *Alfie* series. Hughes has won the Eleanor Farjeon Award, and the Kate Greenaway Medal for Illustration twice. In 1999 she received an OBE for services to children's literature.

Nicholas Hytner is the Director of the National Theatre, and a theatre, film and opera director. Under his stewardship, the multi-award winning stage adaptation of Michael Morpurgo's novel *War Horse* was first staged at the National Theatre. He was knighted for services to drama in 2010.

Jeremy Irvine is an actor. He played Albert Narracott in Steven Spielberg's 2011 film adaptation of Michael Morpurgo's novel *War Horse*. A keen amateur historian, Irvine has carried out extensive research into the life of Albert Ball since discovering his story whilst filming *War Horse*, and has written about the fighter pilot's extraordinary life.

Catherine Johnson is an author and screenwriter. She has written several novels for children and young adults, and co-wrote the screenplay for the 2004 film *Bullet Boy*. She held the position of Writer in Residence at Holloway Prison, and Royal Literary Fund Writing Fellow at the London Institute, and has mentored African writers in association with the British Council.

Michael Longley has published nine collections of poetry, including *Gorse Fires* (1991), which won the Whitbread Poetry Award, and *The Weather in Japan* (2000), which won the Hawthornden Prize, the T. S. Eliot Prize and the Irish Times Poetry Prize. In 2001 he received the Queen's Gold Medal for

Poetry, and in 2003 the Wilfred Owen Award. His new collection, *The Stairwell*, is published this year. He was awarded a CBE in 2010.

Joanna Lumley is an actress, voice-over artist and author. Lumley is an outspoken human rights activist and is an advocate for a number of charities and animal welfare groups. She received an OBE in 1995. She has published a number of memoirs; her most recent, *Absolutely*, was published in 2011.

Michelle Magorian is an author of children's books, best known for her first novel, *Goodnight Mister Tom*, which won the 1982 Guardian Children's Fiction Prize and has been adapted for stage and screen. Her novel *Just Henry* won the Costa Children's Book Award in 2008.

Simon Mayo is a broadcaster and author. Mayo is the current presenter of *Drivetime* on BBC Radio 2, and also the co-presents *Kermode and Mayo's Film Review* on BBC Radio 5 Live. He is the author of the Itch series of books for young readers.

Roger McGough is a poet, performer, children's author and play-wright. He presents *Poetry Please* on BBC Radio 4 and is President of the Poetry Society. A Freeman of the City of Liverpool, he was awarded a CBE in 2004 for services to literature.

Virginia McKenna is an actress, author and wildlife campaigner. McKenna is Co-Founder and Trustee of the Born Free Foundation, an international conservation charity, and supports and is patron of many other charities. She has written books for children and adults. She was awarded an OBE for her services to conservation and the arts in 2004.

Clare Morpurgo, mother of three, grandmother of eight, is the Founder of Farms for City Children, an educational charity that, since its foundation in 1976, has enabled over 100,000 urban children to live and work on one of the charity's three farms for a week of their young lives. She is co-author with Michael of *Where My Wellies Take Me*, and has worked with him on his books, and with Farms for City Children, for over forty years.

Kate Mosse is the award-winning author of the Languedoc Trilogy – *Labyrinth, Sepulchre and Citadel* – as well as four works of non-fiction, three plays and three Gothic novels, including *The Taxidermist's Daughter*, published in September 2014. The Co-Founder & Chair of the Board of the Baileys Women's Prize for Fiction (previously the Orange Prize), she is on the board of the National Theatre, the Executive Committee of Women of the World and is a Patron of the Sussex early music ensemble, The Consort of Twelve. She was appointed an OBE for services to women and to literature in 2013.

Sir Andrew Motion is a poet, novelist and biographer, and was Poet Laureate from 1999 to 2009. He has received numerous awards for his poetry and has published four celebrated biographies, including the authorized life of Philip Larkin, which won the Whitbread Prize for Biography. He was knighted for his services to poetry in 2009.

Cathy Newman presents Channel 4 News. She spent nearly a decade in Fleet Street, latterly with the Financial Times. Since joining Channel 4 News, she has broadcast a string of investigations and high-profile scoops. She also writes about politics for the *Daily Telegraph*.

Brian Patten came to prominence in the 1960s as one of the Liverpool Poets. He co-wrote the seminal poetry anthology, *The*

Mersey Sound. He has published many acclaimed poetry collections for children and adults. He has been honoured with the Freedom of the City of Liverpool and is a Fellow of the Royal Society of Literature and of both Liverpool University and John Moores University.

K. M. Peyton is the author of over seventy novels for children and adults. She wrote the much-loved *Flambards* series, for which she won the 1969 Carnegie Medal and the 1970 Guardian Children's Fiction Prize. In 1979 her *Flambards* trilogy was adapted as a thirteen-part television series.

James Patterson is the author of some of the most popular series of the past decade, as well as many other bestsellers; including romance novels and stand-alone thrillers. Inspired by his own son, who was a reluctant reader, he also writes a range of books specifically for young readers. James is a founding partner of Booktrust's Children's Reading Fund in the UK. In 2010 he was voted Author of the Year at the Children's Choice Book Awards in New York.

Sir Jonathon Porritt is an environmentalist and writer promoting conservation and sustainable development. He is the Founder and Director of Forum for the Future, Chairman of the UK Sustainable Development Commission, and author of a number of books on Green issues, including the novel, *The World We Made*. He was awarded a CBE in 2000.

Sir Terry Pratchett is the acclaimed creator of the global bestselling Discworld® series. He is the author of fifty bestselling novels, many of which have been adapted for stage and screen. His books have won many awards, including the Carnegie Medal, and he was awarded a knighthood for services to literature in 2008.

Bali Rai has written numerous books for children and young adults. His first, *(un)arranged marriage*, won many awards, including the Angus Book Award and the Leicester Book of the Year. It was also shortlisted for the prestigious Branford Boase first novel award. *Rani and Sukh* and *The Whisper* were both shortlisted for the Booktrust Teenage Prize.

Dame Gail Rebuck is Chair of the UK arm of Penguin Random House, the world's biggest publisher. Rebuck was previously Chief Executive of Random House Group UK, a position she held for twenty-three years. In 2001 she received a CBE, and in 2009 was made a Dame.

Chris Riddell is an artist, illustrator and author of children's books, and political cartoonist for the *Observer*. His books have won many awards, including the 2001 and 2004 Kate Greenaway Medals, the 2007 Nestlé Smarties Book Prize and the 2013 Costa Children's Book Award.

Sir Tony Robinson is an actor, comedian, historian and television presenter. He is known for playing Baldrick in the popular television sitcom *Blackadder* and was host of the archaeology series *Time Team*. Robinson has written many books for children and has narrated the audiobooks of Terry Pratchett's Discworld® novels. In 2013 he was knighted for public and political service.

Meg Rosoff is an author. Her first book, How I Live Now, won the Guardian Children's Fiction Prize, the Printz Award, and the Branford Boase Award, and her second, Just in Case, won the Carnegie Medal in 2006. Her latest book, Picture Me Gone, was shortlisted for the National Book Awards in the USA.

Nick Sharratt has written and illustrated more than forty books for children. He has illustrated around 250 titles for several top children's authors, most notably Jacqueline Wilson. He has won numerous prizes for his work, and was the official World Book Day illustrator in 2006.

Helen Skelton is a broadcaster, and presented *Blue Peter* from 2008 to 2013. In 2010 she kayaked the length of the Amazon for Sport Relief, and in 2011 walked a tightrope between the towers of Battersea Power Station for Comic Relief. She was only the second woman to complete the Namibian Ultra-Marathon, and was the first person to reach the South Pole by bicycle. Her first book for children is published in 2015.

Jon Snow is a journalist and broadcaster. He presents *Channel 4 News* and has travelled the globe covering world events. Snow was Chancellor of Oxford Brookes University from 2001 to 2008, and has received many awards for his journalism, including the Richard Dimbleby BAFTA award for Best Factual Contribution to Television.

Rory Stewart is a diplomat, traveller, author and MP for Penrith and the Borders. His account of crossing Afghanistan on foot, *The Places in Between*, was an international bestseller. *Occupational Hazards* describes his work in Iraq. In 2005 he established the charity Turquoise Mountain in Kabul.

Jonathan Stroud is an author who writes for children and young adults. He is the author of the bestselling *Bartimaeus* sequence, which is published in thirty-six languages and won the Mythopoeic Fantasy Award for Children's Literature (2006), the Corinne Award in Germany (2006) and the Grand Prix de l'Imaginaire (2007). His new series, *Lockwood & Co.*, launched in 2013 to critical acclaim and eleven literary award shortlistings.

Emma Thompson is an actress, comedian, screenwriter and author. She is the only person to have received Academy Awards for both acting and writing, winning the award for Best Actress for *Howards End* in 1992, and the award for Best Adapted Screenplay for *Sense and Sensibility* in 1995. In 2012 Thompson wrote *The Further Tale of Peter Rabbit* to celebrate the 110th anniversary of the publication of Beatrix Potter's *The Tale of Peter Rabbit*.

Alan Titchmarsh is a horticulturalist and broadcaster. He is the author of over fifty books about gardening, several memoirs, and nine novels. He writes for the *Sunday Telegraph, Country Life* and *BBC Gardeners' World* magazine, is the gardening correspondent of the *Daily Express* and *Sunday Express*, and presents a regular show on Classic FM. He was appointed MBE in 2000.

Sandi Toksvig is a writer, presenter, comedian, actress and producer. She has written more than twenty books for both children and adults. She hosts both radio and television shows including, *The News Quiz* on BBC radio. In October 2012 she was made Chancellor of the University of Portsmouth, and in 2014 received an OBE for services to broadcasting.

Dr Rowan Williams is a theologian, poet and author. Williams stepped down from his position as 104th Archbishop of Canterbury on 31 December 2012 and became Master of Magdalene College, Cambridge, in January 2013. He is the author on several books of theology and a frequent broadcaster.

Dame Jacqueline Wilson is a children's author who served as Children's Laureate from 2005 to 2007. Her books have won many awards and her bestselling titles include *The Story of Tracy Beaker* and the *Hetty Feather* trilogy. She has been awarded both an OBE and a DBE. Her 100th novel will be published in 2014.

Caroline Wyatt has been a correspondent and occasional presenter for *BBC News* for over twenty years. Wyatt joined the BBC in 1991 and became Defence Correspondent in October 2007, and has covered the wars in Kosovo, Chechnya, Georgia, Iraq and Afghanistan. She is a contributor to *The Oxford Handbook of War*.

ACKNOWLEDGEMENTS

Prose and poetry

Pat Barker, *Regeneration* (Penguin Books Ltd, 1992), copyright © Pat Barker, 1991. Reprinted by permission of Penguin Books Ltd.

Edmund Blunden, 'Can You Remember?' from *Selected Poems* (Carcanet, 1982). Reprinted by permission of Carcanet Press Limited.

John Boyne, *Stay Where You Are and Then Leave* (Doubleday, 2013), copyright © John Boyne, 2013. Reprinted by permission of The Random House Group Limited.

Theresa Breslin, *Ghost Soldier* (Doubleday, 2014), copyright © Theresa Breslin, 2014. Reprinted by permission of The Random House Group Limited.

Raymond Briggs, 'Aunties', copyright © Raymond Briggs, 2014.

Vera Brittain, *Testament of Youth* (Victor Gollancz, 1933). Included by permission of Mark Bostridge and T. J. Brittain-Catlin, Literary Executors for the Vera Brittain Estate 1970.

Duff Cooper, diary excerpts, copyright © John Julius Norwich, 2014.

Jilly Cooper, *Animals in War* (Corgi, 1984), copyright © Jilly Cooper, 1984. Reprinted by permission of The Random House Group Limited.

Richard Curtis and Ben Elton, 'Good-bye-ee' from *Blackadder Goes Forth*, original script copyright © Richard Curtis and Ben Elton, 1989. The programme based on this script first shown by BBC Television in 1989.

George Davison diary entries, copyright © Jonathan Stroud, 2014.

Carol Ann Duffy, 'Last Post' from *The Bees* (Picador, 2011), copyright © Carol Ann Duffy, 2011. *The Christmas Truce* (Picador, 2011), copyright © Carol Ann Duffy, 2011 – Reproduced by permission of the author c/o Rogers, Coleridge & White Ltd, 20 Powis Mews, London W11 1JN.

Eleanor Farjeon, 'Easter Monday (In Memoriam E. T.)' from *First and Second Love* (Michael Joseph, 1947). Reproduced by kind permission of the Miss E. Farjeon Wills Trust.

Sebastian Faulks, *Birdsong* (Hutchinson, 1993), copyright © Sebastian

Images and illustrations